THE ABSOLUTE UNIQUENESS
OF
MONSIGNOR ALFRED GILBEY

The Absolute Uniqueness *of* MONSIGNOR ALFRED GILBEY

The Final Interview
With extensive end-notes and appendices

ALEXANDER HAYDON
Foreword by Christopher Monckton

AROUCA
PRESS

Arouca Press, Waterloo N2J 0A5
© 2025 by Alexander Haydon
www.aroucapress.com

All rights reserved:
No part of this book may be reproduced or transmitted,
in any form or by any means, without permission.

ISBN: 978-1-998492-36-7 (pbk)
ISBN: 978-1-998492-37-4 (hc)

To my mother and father
with undying love

Requiescant in pace

CONTENTS

Foreword *by Christopher Monckton of Brenchley* xxi
Author's Note xxvii
Acknowledgments. xxviii
Preface: The Life and Death of a Great Priest xxxi

THE FINAL INTERVIEW 1

PART 1: The Faith 3
   Questions 1 and 2: The Foundation of Faith in Reason 5
   Questions 3 to 7: Divine Revelation 7
   Questions 8 and 9: Jesus Christ, God Incarnate 13
   Question 10: The Visible Church. 14

PART 2: Controversies 19
   Questions 1 and 2: Why He Resigned 19
   Question 3: Counsels and Commandments. 27
   Question 4: The Poor in Spirit 34
   Question 5: The Third World and the Next World 38
   Question 6: Tax Avoidance and Tax Evasion 40
   Question 7: The Last Days. 43
   Question 8: A New Dark Age. 44
   Question 9: Sex Education. 48
   Question 10: Contraception: Conscientious Objection? 52
   Question 11: Contraception: Why Artificial is Wrong,
      but Natural O.K.. 54
   Question 12: Mortal Beauty 55
   Question 13: The Role of Feeling in Religion 56
   Question 14: Jesus Christ in Clubland. 57
   Question 15: The History of Cruelty in the Church 58
   Question 16: His Happiest Moment 61

PART 3: Appendices. 79
   APPENDIX I: Alfred and Franco. 79
   APPENDIX II: Alfred Against the Modernists. 89
   APPENDIX III: The Marlborough Annulment 93
   APPENDIX IV: *Humanae Vitae*: Pope Paul's Prophetic Words . . 96
   APPENDIX V: Church Teaching & World Population:
      God's Truth and A Persistent Myth 99
   Bibliography 107

Truth alone is worthy of our entire devotion.
 —FR VINCENT MCNABB OP
 (1868–1943), epigraph to *We Believe*.

Mgr Ronald Knox (1888–1957), whose chaplaincy at Oxford (1926–1939) overlapped with Alfred's (1933–65), said of McNabb: 'Father Vincent is the only person I have ever known about whom I have felt…"He gives you some idea of what a saint must be like."' Many, including the author, could say the same of Alfred Gilbey. I would apply the description also to the not dissimilar Fr Jean-Marie Charles-Roux IC (1914–2014).

God has created me to do Him some definite service; He has committed some work to me which He has not committed to another…I am a link in a chain, a bond of connection between persons.
 —SAINT JOHN HENRY NEWMAN
 Meditations and Devotions, 1848

The function of the Church in every Age has been conservative—to transmit undiminished and uncontaminated the creed inherited from its predecessors. Not 'is this fashionable notion one that we should accept?' but 'is this dogma the Faith as we received it?' has been the question at all General Councils.
 —EVELYN WAUGH
 Essays, 629, quoted in *The Sayings of Evelyn Waugh*, ed. Donat Gallagher, 1996.

Fig. 1: Alfred's parents, c. 1910.

Fig. 2: Young Alfred in cassock, c. 1930.

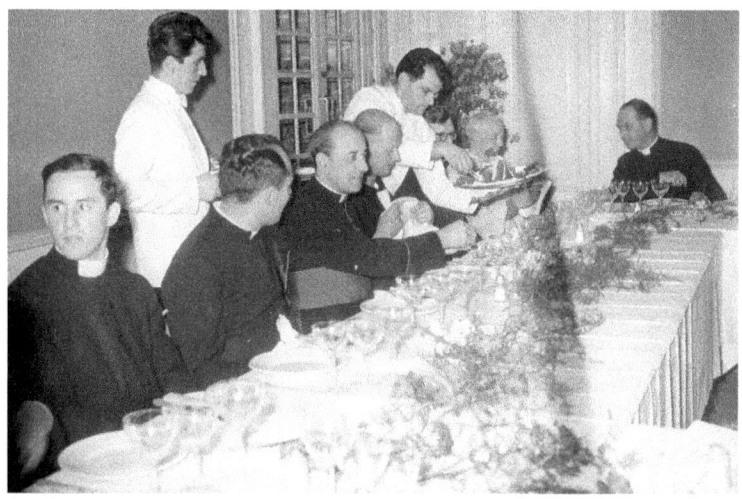

Fig. 3: Alfred at banquet with fellow priests, 1940s.
Copyright Pontificia Fotografia G. Felici.

Fig. 4: Alfred at same banquet with fellow priests, 1940s.
Copyright Pontificia Fotografia G. Felici.

Fig. 5: Alfred at same banquet with fellow priests, 1940s.
Copyright Pontificia Fotografia G. Felici.

Fig. 6: Alfred with newly-weds, 1950s.
Copyright Daphne McLeod.

Fig. 7: Alfred with clergy group on special occasion, c. 1960.
Copyright Mayfair Studios.

Fig. 8: Alfred with fellow Cambridge Chaplains, all wearing different clothes: from L to R: Fr Christopher Jenkins, Mgr Richard Incledon, Alfred, Fr Francis Selman, Archbishop Couve de Murville, 1980s.
Courtesy of Alan Robinson (St Edmund's College, Ware).

Fig. 9: Alfred reading, 1980s.

Fig. 10: Alfred in full fig, in a library, 1990s.

Fig. 11: Alfred, 1990s.
Courtesy of Alan Robinson (St Edmund's College, Ware).

Fig. 12: Alfred with Margaret Ross Williamson
at her flat shortly before his 94th birthday, June 1995.

Fig. 13: Private chapel at Alfred's cousin's house, Rose Hill, Henley, made from an engine room, used for a monthly Sunday Mass. Courtesy of Alan Robinson (St Edmund's College, Ware).

Fig. 14: Archway leading into entrance courtyard at Fisher House, Cambridge. Courtesy of Alan Robinson (St Edmund's College, Ware).

> TRAVELLERS' CLUB,
> LONDON, S.W.1.
>
> *Friday of this week is the first Friday of the month. By the kindness of the Fathers of the Society I shall be celebrating Mass in the Sodality Chapel, 114, Mount Street, London, W.1. that evening at 6.30 p.m.*
>
> *For the benefit of those who find Friday inconvenient I shall also be saying Mass on the immediately previous Thursday evening at the same time and place.*
>
> *On both these evenings I shall be hearing confessions in the parlour on the ground floor for half-an-hour before Mass.*
>
> A. N. GILBEY

Fig. 15: Alfred's regular invitation to his monthly
First Friday Mass at British Jesuit HQ in London.
Courtesy of Alan Robinson (St Edmund's College, Ware).

> ✝
>
> In thanksgiving for my ordination
>
> to the priesthood on the
>
> Feast of the Assumption
>
> 15th August
>
> **1929**
>
> **ALFRED NEWMAN GILBEY**
>
> **1979**
>
> Please pray for me

Fig. 16: Alfred's card of thanksgiving for
the fiftieth anniversary of his ordination, 1979.
Courtesy of Alan Robinson (St Edmund's College, Ware).

FOREWORD
Christopher Monckton of Brenchley

ALFRED NEWMAN GILBEY, WERE HE STILL among us, would have smiled upon Alex Haydon's last interview of him as his own *Apologia pro vita sua*. Certainly, he was so fascinated by the project that he invited Alex to visit him on a dozen occasions so that the work could be completed. In questioning Alfred, Alex pulled no punches. Yet Alfred—a cheerful controversialist who liked nothing better than an amiable Aquinian *disputatio*—seems to have relished the experience. The resulting interview, then, is a searching, and sometimes searing, examination of the soul and conscience of one of Britain's best-loved priests.

I first met Alfred when, at the age of three weeks, I decided to join the Catholic Church. My late father had reached the same decision before going up to Cambridge shortly before World War II. He had once told me, in his soldierly way, that if one was going to be religious at all then one must be Catholic. On going up to Cambridge, he met Alfred, was given 20 hour-long tutorials in the Faith, was received into the Church and was swiftly disinherited by his wealthy Scots Presbyterian maternal grandfather, who, during the solemn moment of consecration at my father's wedding (at which Alfred presided), was heard to say, "What are those damned cow-bells for?"

When I went to Cambridge I saw Alfred at least once a term, usually at the amiable dinners of the Strafford Club, founded by him in honour of Thomas Wentworth, First Earl of Strafford. Some years thereafter I became Editor of the Fleet Street weekly Catholic newspaper *The Universe*, and learned from priests and parishes that what they wanted was a weekly course of instruction in the Faith. At the same time, I visited Peterhouse to attend a College feast at the invitation of Professor Adrian Mathias, the world's foremost mathematical logician.

At the time, Adrian had just completed his own 20 hours' instruction in the Faith at Alfred's hands and had recently been baptized. He had realized at the outset that Alfred's words were a *monumentum aere perennius.* He had tape-recorded all the sessions and had arranged for them to be transcribed by the College secretary. The combination of the blessed mutter of the Monsignor, whose diction was famously indistinct, and the secretary's unfamiliarity with the complexities of theological vocabulary produced an untidy and often hilarious manuscript. The "Marxist Fathers" made an appearance at one point.

On reading the manuscript, however, I saw that Adrian was right. It was exceptional. I edited and retyped the entire manuscript, correcting the errors and doing a little restructuring. Alfred then corrected it, and asked whether I could arrange for it to receive the official *Imprimatur* of the Church.

The very next week, I was due to visit the late Bishop Thomas Holland of Salford, who lived in a small stately home curiously located in the middle of a motorway roundabout, from which he could reach all parts of his diocese within minutes. I mentioned Alfred's manuscript to the Bishop, who said he would pass it to his *censor deputatus* for attention.

However, like me, the Bishop, England's most formidable theologian, became so captivated by Alfred's work that he read the whole manuscript himself. After very few corrections, he granted the *Imprimatur* personally. *The Universe* ran Alfred's course as a weekly series, and the circulation soared from 110,000 to 160,000 in just three years.

In Alfred's interview, you will find many references to the resulting book, *We Believe*. I had suggested it should be called *What we believe*, but Alfred, in his mischievous way, said it amused him to take the words "We believe..." from the beginning of the English mistranslation of the opening word *Credo* of the Nicene Creed in the *Novus Ordo Missae*.

Alfred did not live to see the abandonment of that dismal, ugly and often heretical original Gas Board "English" translation, in which the inaccuracies were most frequent wherever uniquely Catholic doctrine was expressed. The Ordinary of the Mass contained some 400 errors for which I would have lost at least half a mark at Cambridge, and the errors clustered whenever the Real Presence was mentioned. I later discovered that the priest in charge of the International Commission on English in the Liturgy had his doubts about the Real Presence, and that very few of the translators were scholars of any merit.

I attended one of their sessions, at which a particular Latin phrase was giving difficulty and had, I suspected, been incorrectly translated. I consulted the dictionary on the table and found, as I had expected, that the phrase was a *hapax legomenon* — a single instance with an idiomatic meaning. I read out what the phrase actually meant. However, Fr John E. Rotelle, the American Augustinian friar in charge of the project, said: "Gee, we already did that bit. Let's move on." That summed up ICEL's approach in those unhappy days.

At *The Universe*, we conducted a survey of the readers. Some 15,000 replied (about one in ten of the circulation). Two-thirds said they would rather have the Tridentine Mass that Alfred said throughout his life. The strength of feeling was palpable. Archbishop Bruno Heim, then the Apostolic Nuncio in England and Wales, contacted me to say that the Holy See had taken serious note of the results of the survey and would in due course arrange for the Mass to be retranslated and the heresies excised. Sure enough, some decades later, the original, lamentable translation was replaced with a worthier, more accurate and less unbeautiful version.

"What scholar-poet," said Douglas Woodruff, commenting on the original translation, "saw fit to render *A solis ortu usque ad occasum* as 'From East to West'?" Now it is, as it should be, "From the rising of the Sun to its setting", poetically celebrating the splendour of Creation.

The Bishops were furious at the result of *The Universe's* survey, for they had recently told the Holy See that everyone in these islands was delighted with the Pidgin-English original version of the *Novus Ordo*. Alfred, however, was fascinated and delighted, for, he said, the result confirmed his prejudice to the effect that the Faithful were more faithful than the hierarchy knew.

Alfred had good reason to know what the Faithful thought: for, during his 100 terms at Fisher House, the Catholic chaplaincy, from which he was cruelly cast out by the modernists just months before he was due to retire anyway, he had received 800 undergraduates, dons and others into the Church. Of these, 80 had become priests. This was a signal achievement. "By their fruits ye shall know them," said the Lord of Life. Alfred's fruits are the priests and laymen now marching merrily in the army of light and truth because it was through him that the Holy Spirit called them. As Alex Haydon recounts, so clear, so authoritative, so elegant, so forceful is *We Believe* that it continues to win souls to this day. Alfred continues his work of conversion from beyond the grave. If every priest had recruited so many to the Faith as had Alfred, the world's Catholic population would be greater by some 350,000,000 souls: an astonishing 25% increase.

Alex's interview of Alfred is in two parts. The first concerns the Faith. The second is a no-holds-barred, no-Queensbury-rules consideration of the numerous controversies arising from Alfred's life and work.

He begins by asking Alfred the question of questions, which Pontius Pilate asked rhetorically at the trial of Christ: "What is the truth?" Alfred replies: "It's not a subjective thing at all … to make up a definition, it is the assertion of a reality outside oneself which one believes corresponds to fact." A purist might take issue with that definition of objective truth: for that which is true is true *in se*, whether you or I or anyone believe it to be true or wish it to be true.

However, Alfred goes on elegantly to straddle the abyss between scientific truths "deduced by a purely intellectual process" and religious truths "obtainable only by faith". It is this fine and apparently effortless reasoning that so mesmerized Adrian Mathias and all of Alfred's 800 converts. It is the absolute, unhesitating, unwavering certitude of Alfred's own personal belief in all that the Church teaches that communicated itself to all who had the joy of sitting at his feet.

Recently, I visited an eminent Professor of science at Oxford at his request to discuss a physical result by my team that he had found, at first blush, to be implausible. "Explain yourself!" he demanded. When I had done so to his satisfaction, he looked up and said, "You know, I can prove scientifically that God does not exist."

"Really?" I replied. "I had thought that, *ex definitione*, science concerned itself not with that which is believed but rather, in Anaximander's words, with the distinction between *to on* and *to me on* — between that which is so and that which is not so."

Despite Max Planck's best efforts, his eponymous constant is nonzero. Therefore, the laws of physics as we now have them did not come into being until, after the Big Bang (first deduced mathematically by a Catholic priest, the Abbé Georges leMaître), the universe had expanded enough to cross the minuscule but nonzero Planck distance. Therefore, the laws of physics could tell us nothing about Who or what created the universe. Besides, the existence of rationally-discernible physical laws at least suggested the possibility of a Lawgiver, just as Hammurabi made the Code of Hammurabi, Solon the Laws of Solon and Justinian the institutes of Justinian. The Professor conceded that he could not, after all, prove the nonexistence of God.

Alfred would have delighted in such a conversation. And here, I think, Holy Mother Church has perhaps missed a trick. For it is now possible to show, by science, that the Church's more contentious moral teachings, which Alfred so cheerfully and unwaveringly upheld and transmitted to his cohort of converts, are objectively speaking right and just. For instance, there was much media muttering about growing national infertility recently when the Office for National Statistics revealed that the indigenous population of these islands is reproducing at a rate of only 1.5 children per lady of child-bearing age, when 2 children are necessary to keep the population stable. Not a single news medium pointed out, however, that in addition to the 600,000 live births last year there were 200,000 abortions. Without that massacre of the innocents, the birthrate would have been exactly sufficient to maintain the population. And, now that it is known to medical science that children in the womb can feel pain, surely it can be agreed that slaughtering them in abattoirs without even giving them the anaesthetics that cattle get constitutes inhuman and degrading punishment at international law.

Reading Alex Haydon's book recalls to mind many such conversations with Alfred, whose humour would intrude even on the weightiest discussions. Once, at dinner at the Travellers' Club, he said he had asked a Spanish waiter named Jesus to identify a member he did not recognize. Jesus had told him at once. Alfred had asked how he knew. The waiter had replied, "Monsignor, Jesus knows everything."

Nothing could better reflect Alfred's method of intellectual discourse than this last interview with Alex Haydon. To those who had the honour to know Alfred as a friend, the book will be a delight. To those who did not meet him, it will be a reminder that our Faith is what the mediaeval schoolmen called a *fides quaerens intellectum* — a system of belief ceaselessly hunting for rational justification. That holy combination of rigorous reasoning and cheerful, unhesitating belief was Alfred Newman Gilbey.

AUTHOR'S NOTE

ALL QUOTATIONS FROM *WE BELIEVE*, ALFRED Gilbey's commentary on the Penny Catechism, are taken from the Gracewing paperback of 2011. The relevant page numbers in the end-notes refer to this edition. Quotations from the Bible are mostly from the Douay-Rheims version (DRC), as revised by Bishop Challoner (1691–1781). This is the Catholic translation, of which the New Testament was first published in 1582, predating the Anglican King James (KJV) version by some 29 years. The Old Testament section of the DRC came out in two parts, in 1609 and 1610. The KJV was published the following year. Those quotations not from the DRC are from the KJV.

ACKNOWLEDGMENTS

AMONG THE MANY HELPFUL PEOPLE, MOSTLY now deceased, who have provided invaluable information and assistance in the writing of this book, and in particular its end-notes and appendices, I should like to single out the following, in alphabetical order (with one exception, at the end of this paragraph): Mrs Joan Bond, Librarian at the Catholic Central Library, Euston (now the Catholic National Library, located at Durham University Library), for her unfailingly cheerful and outstandingly efficient help with various references; the Rt Rev. Bishop Emeritus Patrick Casey (1913–1999) for useful information about Alfred's friend and contemporary the Very Rev. Canon Alfonso de Zulueta (d. 1980); Fr Francis Edwards SJ, Archivist to the Society of Jesus, Farm Street, for tracking down ill-remembered biblical quotations with Jesuitical despatch; Mrs Miriam Fenwick, a helper at St Gregory's Library, the Brompton Oratory, for her wonderfully serene cooperation with all my enquiries on various matters; Miss Joan Gallogly, one of Sr. Brenda's Deputies at Nazareth House, Hammersmith, for key information about Alfred's last two months; the Rev. Brendan Gerard FSSP, then Information Officer, SPUC, for much information always promptly supplied, about abortion, contraception and population; the Very Rev. Canon Richard Incledon (1929–2012), Alfred's immediate successor as Chaplain to the Catholic undergraduates of Cambridge (1965–77), for essential information supplied with exemplary courtesy, including his review of *We Believe*; the Rev. Dom Philip Jebb (1932–2014), Prior of (the now defunct) Downside Abbey, for kindly supplying relevant information from the Downside Archives; Rev. Dom Christopher Jenkins (1932–2003), my wonderful instructor in the Faith, one of Alfred's undergraduate converts, and, as a preacher and apologist, one of his most gifted successors to the Cambridge Chaplaincy (1982–88), for invaluable anecdotes, affectionately told; Sr Brenda McCall, Matron of Nazareth House, Hammersmith, for a vivid account of Alfred's final hours; Dr David J McKitterick, FBA, Librarian, Trinity College, Cambridge, for information about Alfred's undergraduate time at Cambridge; Mgr David Norris, Protonotary Apostolic, Vicar

Acknowledgments xxix

General, Archdiocese of Westminster, for much useful information given with a great, serene sense of humour; Mrs Julie Petrucci, College Secretary, Peterhouse, Cambridge, for useful information about past financial arrangements for undergraduates; Dr David Watkin (1941–2018), FSA, Fellow of Peterhouse, Cambridge, Reader in the History of Architecture (1993–2001), and Literary Executor to Alfred, to whom special thanks are due, for his serious appraisal, warm encouragement and inspiring interest in the venture, as for his prompt supply of recondite information, and last, but by no means least, among the individual helpers, my publisher Alex Barbas, whose warm enthusiasm for the book, combined with his unwaveringly cheerful encouragement, kept me going hopefully throughout the sometimes challenging process of preparing it for publication.

Finally, without knowing their names, I am very grateful for varied and interesting snippets of information, supplied by several members of the Press Office at Archbishop's House, Westminster; certain monks of Belmont Abbey; a member of staff at the British Library, and a member of staff at the Royal Ascot Office.

Without exception those thanked have been unfailingly patient, courteous and helpful, as if the mere mention of Alfred Gilbey brought out the best in them. Even though, in several cases, I have not actually quoted these sources, their combined cornucopia of background information has given me an invaluable perspective on Alfred, enabling me to have a fully rounded picture of the man. To have such assistance was a great blessing, for which, finally I thank Almighty God.

PREFACE

The Life and Death of a Great Priest

*Requiem aeternam dona ei, Domine,
et lux perpetua luceat ei.*

WHILE THE SOLEMN CHANT OF REQUIEM echoed from the sunlit dome above, Fr Ronald Creighton-Jobe, vested largely in black, offered the Holy Sacrifice at the high altar, assisted by two of his brother Oratorians. The eyes of the congregation drank in the scarlet of the Cardinal's robes. Unusually, these were surmounted by a rochet (a kind of mini-surplice) and mozzetta (a little cape about the shoulders) trimmed with white fur in mediaeval style. Gathered around Cardinal Hume, the purple of half a dozen bishops complemented and set off his solitary red flame. The officiating priests were served by a little group of Knights of Malta, whose distinctive large white cross shone bright on their black-robed breasts. A solemn squad of them, likewise habited, filled four rows of seats not far from the altar. Ahead of them sat rank on rank of black-cassocked clerics. A smattering of monks and friars, and a handful of nuns, added here and there a splash of white or brown. The carved dark wood of the polished pulpit gleamed in empty silence. There was no address, no homily. The grand operatic ritual, in all its awesome power, was far more potent than any panegyric.

On the coffin, which was draped in a black pall emblazoned with a large gold cross, (the three-starred coat of arms of St Philip Neri, the founder of the Oratory, in its four corners), stood the mitre and mozzetta to which Alfred Gilbey's status as a Protonotary Apostolic (an honorary prelate) entitled him. The stately ritual, something like a sombre coronation in miniature, drew to its conclusion. Gravely, the cardinal processed down the aisle towards the coffin and intoned: '*Non intres in judicium cum servo tuo Domine*'... ('Enter not into judgement with thy servant, O Lord'). Fr Ronald prepared the censer. The choir sang the *Kyrie eleison*. After the completion of this plea for mercy, they sang *'Libera me Domine'*... 'Deliver me, Lord, from eternal death in that awful day.' The Cardinal said the *'Paternoster'*, continuing the rest of the prayer in silence, walking around the coffin, sprinkling it with holy water and incensing it. There followed a few versicles and responses. Then came the absolution: *'Deus cui proprium est'*... 'O God whose property is ever to have mercy'...

Then the aged bones were borne, with stately dignity, down the long aisle of the grand church towards the great doors, flung wide open to the polluted Knightsbridge air.

Alfred Newman Gilbey was taking his leave for the last time from the building in which, for the last 31 years, he had offered every morning the Holy Sacrifice of the Mass. For one short but glorious hour the Counter-reformation had seemed to breathe again. The crowd in the church that left standing room only had just attended the first public celebration there of a sung solemn requiem Mass in the old Tridentine rite since 1963. It had taken the form laid down for a member of the Order of Malta, of which Alfred was a chaplain of the highest rank. His coffin was driven away in a very grand hearse of 1930s vintage.

He was finally laid to rest beneath the paving-stones of the courtyard of Fisher House in the centre of Cambridge. His body lies where he ministered to the souls of undergraduates, graduates and dons from 1932 to 1965. Fittingly, he had said in 1947 when the City Council was planning to demolish the chaplaincy to make way for a modern development, that it would only happen over his dead body.

We Believe, the book which grew out of the course of instruction he gave to enquirers, had by the time of his death, in A. N. Wilson's words 'acquired a legendary status', and had inspired over forty vocations to the priesthood and religious life. But it was not his book alone, but also the extraordinary example and charisma of his life and personality that attracted those with these vocations. In spite of his outwardly comfortable lifestyle, Alfred imposed certain mortifications on himself. For example, he restricted himself to one course at dinner and usually only one glass of wine, allowing his guests to finish off the rest of the bottle. He also used, as his young friend Charles des Forges discovered when packing up his belongings for his final move from the Travellers to Nazareth House, 'a discipline and a spiky belt.'[1] I, for one, am convinced that he was a saint. I know I am not alone in this, and I hope and pray he will be canonised as soon as possible, so that his teaching and example may liberate people from the curse of egalitarianism and enable them to focus on the pursuit of their own unique vocation, which only they can fulfil, whatever it may be. 'By their fruits ye shall know them.'[2]

In 1965, the same year that he resigned from the chaplaincy, Alfred took up residence first at the Athenaeum, from which for two or three months he commuted every ten days to the Travellers Club, as there was a limit on the number of nights one could stay at either. After a while he was granted permission to live at the Travellers, becoming the club's only resident member. There, in the former boot-room at the top of the rickety staircase that led up from the old-fashioned cast-iron lift, he set up a tiny chapel, with his collection of relics displayed on the altar. Here he said Mass. He also said the Rosary every day there, kneeling at his prie-dieu. Just above the fat pipes that heated the club, it was sometimes stiflingly hot, as I remember from several visits. On these occasions, I felt immensely privileged and blessed to be saying the Rosary with a priest of such manifest holiness, especially as he always said, once the final bead had been told: 'Jesus, convert England. Jesus, give back the Faith to Wales. Jesus, have mercy on this country.' One felt that in joining with him in this prayer one was, in a tiny way, helping in the eventual return of our country to Holy Mother Church.

Every morning at seven o'clock he said Mass at the Brompton Oratory,[3] except on Thursdays, when he said it at the club at half past six in the evening, sometimes alone, but often to a handful of friends and acquaintances, or to anyone who happened to drop in. In addition, at the same time on the first Friday of every month and 'for the benefit of those who find Friday evening inconvenient', as he said on his printed invitations, on the Thursday preceding it, he heard confessions and said Mass in the little sodality chapel at the British headquarters of the Society of Jesus, Farm Street, Mayfair.

Unless he had a pressing engagement, these Farm Street Masses would be followed by a visit to the Running Footman, and latterly the Bunch of Grapes, both nearby pubs. Here, familiar to the regulars in his clerical frock-coat, he would enjoy a glass or two of sherry. The vast majority of those attending were men, many being members of his old Cambridge flock, though there were usually also a handful of women, some of whom had met him while studying at Cambridge when he went back there on frequent visits long after his days of chaplaincy.

Alfred lived at the Travellers Club until shortly before his death. Eventually, due to the gradually increasing decline of his formerly excellent health, having had several falls, on January 31, 1998, he was put into the hands of the Poor Sisters of Nazareth at their home for retired priests in Hammersmith. There, on March 26, he suffered a heart-attack in the bathroom at about six o'clock in the morning. The Matron, Sister Brenda, took him straight to Charing Cross Hospital, but he died shortly afterwards, fortified by the rites of Holy Church. He had continued to say his seven o'clock morning Mass right up to the last: he had offered the Holy Sacrifice for the last time the morning before, on the feast of the Annunciation.

I was first introduced to Monsignor Alfred Newman Gilbey, Protonotary Apostolic, Domestic Prelate to His Holiness, Grand Cross Conventual Chaplain *ad honorem* to the Knights of Malta, Chaplain to the Catholic undergraduates of Cambridge 1932–65, in 1986. As an undergraduate then myself, I had been invited to a breakfast given at Fisher House, the chaplaincy building, after attending Mass said by him in the chapel. My first impression of this aged priest was that there could not be anyone else quite like him in the world. Alfred's bubbling, chuckling gaiety and gentle humour, his gracefully formal, chivalric courtesy, his sparkling and alert delight in the conversation of the undergraduates around him, all of them at least sixty years younger than he, his passionate interest in the project of one of them, Madeleine Beard, who was writing a book on the great country houses of Britain (*Acres and Heirlooms: the Survival of Britain's Historic Estates,* 1989), his flamboyant elegance: all these made up the shiny shell around a kernel of true holiness. At the age of 84, he fizzed like vintage champagne. I did not then grasp that his wonderful ease and serenity flowed from the rock of his absolute certitude in the Faith, the rock of Peter, nor how deep was the passionate love he had for Christ and his Church. On closer acquaintance, and especially on reading his classic work of apologetic, *We Believe*, then a new book that had been published three years before, anonymously, 'by a priest', this struck me with great force.

Our host was the then chaplain, Dom Christopher Jenkins (1932–2003), a monk of Belmont Abbey, himself an undergraduate convert of Alfred's. Before the breakfast, we had attended Mass said by Alfred in the chapel of Fisher House. For me, as a very recent convert, this was my first experience of the old Latin Mass. It started with the unmistakable presence of the venerable priest as, wearing one of the most gorgeous embroidered chasubles and an intricately woven cream-coloured lacework alb, he shuffled purposefully up to the new table-style altar, genuflected slowly and, with a graceful movement, placed his black biretta, with its purple tuft, on the altar steps. Then began 'the blessed mutter.'[4] Its elegant formalism, his hieratic manner, contrasting with the ugliness of the cheaply carpeted and rubber-edged altar steps, recalled a Shinto rite.

This was the Mass as it had been said throughout the Western Catholic Church for four centuries, from the promulgation of the Tridentine missal by Pope St Pius V in 1570, to that introduced in the wake of the Second Vatican Council in 1969. How, I wondered, could this old priest defy the changes authorised by popes in concert with the bishops of the Church in a General Council? As he himself had written in *We Believe*:

> As a Catholic one obeys laws within the Church, whether one agrees with them or not, so long as one does not believe them to be sinful.
>
> Take the liturgical changes through which we have been passing. Many people may have found them distasteful, others desirable, but there is no question that you must obey them. You cannot go along your own way in withstanding the authority of the Church.[5]

And as he was to comment in the interview he gave me for the *Catholic Herald* in April 1996:

> I'm not saying the vernacular [Mass] is wrong. I'm a loyal subject of the Church, and the Church orders the liturgy as she thinks desirable. Well, bear this in mind, if anyone

doubt my orthodoxy: I don't myself desire the change, and I have the privilege of following the old use — but that is not the same thing as saying, as some extremists do, 'The new is not valid.'

Of course it is! What the Church says authenticates it. But I think that the changes have made the most frightful chaos of the one holy Catholic Church, and have caused great suffering to many people. But she's still the one holy Catholic Church. There's no other, and all authority resides in her.

'I have the privilege of following the old use.' This was a dispensation granted to a handful of priests who felt unable to accept the new rite of the Mass. It was also enjoyed by the well-known London Rosminian Fr Jean-Marie Charles-Roux,[6] a sort of alternative gallic Gilbey, at St Etheldreda's, Holborn, and by Fr Gerard Corr at the Servites' church in Fulham. As Alfred had stressed in another of his manifold interviews: 'I am not a rebel.' Anyone who knew him would scarcely need such reassurance! This gentlest of gentlemen would never have dreamt of challenging the authority of the Church he loved, the Church in which, as he wrote 'we believe that the Incarnation of Christ continues.'[7] What he would have done if he had not been granted the dispensation from saying the new rite one cannot say, but to imagine him pronouncing the words of consecration in English is inconceivable!

'The privilege of following the old use.' To me this phrase sums up Alfred's attitude to life in general. By the time I met him, of course, the mere fact of his age might well have made one think his antiquated ways and manners, like his Victorian mode of dress, with his shovel hat, flyless breeches, double-waisted waistcoat and frock-coat, the nostalgic relics of the time in which he had been brought up. In fact his age disguised the fact that he had chosen as a young man to make himself a living fossil, preserving the sartorial appearance of the Jesuit priest who used to come up from Farm Street every Sunday to say Mass for his parents, their children and their nine servants in their private chapel. He saw no reason to introduce any innovation. Or rather, he ardently wished to preserve that happy world of the Essex mansion, in which his foxhunting father, lovingly married to his devout Spanish wife, had ruled affectionately over little Alfred and his six elder siblings. He was one who never ceased to express his gratitude for the providence which had blessed him with the happiest of starts in life. It is also true, as his friend Peter Gregory-Jones remarks, that 'he had reached sartorial maturity in the early 1920s, when gentlemanly English priests wore clerical frock-coats and black silk waistcoats.'[8]

Alfred enjoyed his many privileges to the full. He never ceased to thank Almighty God for granting them. His parents' house, Mark Hall, near Harlow, burnt down in 1947, much to Alfred's distress (his father, the last Gilbey occupant, had died in 1942). He consoled himself with the thought that it was thus spared association with the ugly modern development which later blighted the area. The same year as the fire, women were at last admitted to undergraduate status at Cambridge. 1947 could thus be seen as an *annus horribilis* for Alfred!

As one of his obituarists wrote, of no one could it be more fittingly said that he was a living fossil. My Catholic Herald interview with him in 1996 billed him as 'the frock-coated hero of the fogey tendency,' and Alfred was certainly a young fogey before he became an old one. He was also a recognisable type of what the Peterhouse historian Maurice Cowling called 'religious dandyism.'[9] If this sprung naturally from his love of elegance, it was also a weapon in the spiritual battle. For many converts, it was the bait.

I shall never forget him on his ninetieth birthday, after two effusive eulogies in a row, one from his friend and first publisher Victor Walne, another from Cardinal Hume, looking a little overcome by the praise that had been poured out on him, as he rose with customary deliberate grace to say that, before anyone else, he wanted to thank his father and mother, 'to whom,' as he put it in the dedication of his Commonplace Book, 'under God, I owe all I have.' He went on to say: 'No man ever had better parents than I.' His was obviously a loving and orderly home. He once told me of sitting as a little boy at the foot of his mother's chair as she led the family in its daily recitation of the Rosary. The scene is reminiscent of the opening of Tomasi de Lampedusa's great novel *The Leopard* (1958), though Alfred would immediately have emphasised, had such a comparison been made to him, that his own stock was somewhat less exalted than that of Prince Don

Fabrizio Salina. But through his mother he was the great-nephew of the Marques de Torre Soto (the head of the Gonzalez sherry family) and, like Alastair Hugh Graham, one of Evelyn Waugh's inspirations for the character of Sebastian Flyte, the nephew of a baronet. He was, indeed, the very incarnation of *noblesse oblige*.

As my father had been a member of his undergraduate flock in the 1950s, Alfred came to my parents' wedding. Because my mother, a nominal Anglican by birth, had felt unpersuaded by the Jesuit instruction she received at Farm Street, there were no wedding bells.[10] This was due to the protocol for 'mixed marriages' in those days. But Alfred arrived in full monsignorial get-up, with scarlet-magenta sash, buttons, and piping. 'I'm here to give it colour!' he said. It was typical of his generous spirit.

Indeed, he felt deeply for those whose childhoods had been marred by abuse, divorce, neglect, or other disorder. In the first chapter of *We Believe*, he writes:

> Think again how many people there are in the world today who are absolutely miserable, questioning their own identity — a disease peculiar to our generation. Many are frequently miserable because they take not Almighty God but their neighbour as their yardstick and feel that they are not wanted, that they have no business to exist.[11]

I saw his compassion for the deficiently loved in the flesh many times, when he listened with great attention and sympathy to all sorts and conditions of men — and, occasionally, of women too. Yet many dismissed him as a reactionary misogynistic snob. He would have felt no sense of shame at being a reactionary, given the meaning of this word: 'a person who holds political views that favour a return to the *status quo ante*, the previous political state of society, which that person believes possessed positive characteristics absent from contemporary society.' As for misogyny, defined as 'feelings of hating women, or the belief that men are much better than women,' although he clearly preferred the company of his own sex, the idea that he had any such thing as hatred of women, or considered men superior to women, is without foundation. Nonetheless, he believed that the sexes were created by God to be *complementary* to one another. As for snobbery, whilst he took a delighted interest in

Preface

such matters as genealogy, the country house life of the gentry and the details of heraldry, to imagine that Alfred really thought less of anybody on the basis of their lower social status would be completely contrary to his profound charity towards every human being as a unique child of Almighty God. But in our triumphantly demotic age a Catholic priest who confidently expressed such unfashionable views and who also had chosen to make his home in a gentlemen's club, could not possibly come to prominence without being misunderstood, caricatured, and treated superficially.

To some degree, any representative of Christ and His Church must expect to suffer calumny at the very least, if he is to exemplify and preach the Gospel to a stiff-necked world. 'If the world hate you, ye know that it hated me before it hated you' (John 15:18). And 'John came neither eating nor drinking, and they say, He hath a devil. The Son of Man came eating and drinking, and they say, Behold a man gluttonous, and a friend of publicans and sinners.' (Matthew 11:18–19).

It is of course true that the great majority of Alfred's flock were men drawn from the professional classes and above. Given his position at Cambridge as well as his chaplaincy to the British Knights of Malta, this could hardly have been otherwise.[12] Some called it 'the apostolate of cocktails.' But, as his convert Dom Christopher Jenkins pointed out: 'Even cocktail drinkers have souls.' Christ Himself dined with the Pharisees.

Yet Alfred Gilbey was criticised by some of his fellow clergy. After I had remarked in his defence to a priest from his own diocese of Brentwood how many people he had drawn into the Church, he expressed a perhaps not uncommon view: 'Yes, but has he converted them to Catholicism or to Gilbeyism?'[13] That remark could be turned back on the questioner to ask him: 'Have you converted your converts to Catholicism as traditionally understood and practised, or to a diluted modernist and egalitarian betrayal of it?' It is undeniable that Alfred's manner of presenting the Faith, with his unembarrassed defence of privilege and hierarchy, was offensive to the egalitarian views of many, if not most, of the clergy of the present-day Church. One commentator described him as a 'saintly snob.' This implies that he looked down on people of lower social standing. I am quite sure this was not so. But of his strong interest in genealogy, heraldry and the aristocracy in general he made no secret. In his own words:

> The widespread superstition that we are all equal in God's sight runs counter to the whole Christian philosophy of life. Equality is observed nowhere in creation: not only is each man absolutely unique, but every leaf of every tree, every pebble on the beach, every grain of sand on the seashore, is unlike any other. There is no sense in which equality exists between them. Furthermore, not only are our physical conditions unique but also our mental and spiritual conditions. Our gifts and defects of character are peculiar to each single one of us.
>
> To say, as a critic may, that Christianity is in favour of inequality is as meaningless as to say that Christianity is in favour of the Law of Gravitation. Christianity accepts that it is so. All attempts to change the nature of things lead to greater suffering than the evils they seek to avoid. They are a sin against the truth.
>
> Some would say at this point, 'Oh, but surely we are all equal in the sight of Almighty God: He loves us all equally.' This is palpably untrue. You cannot imagine that Our Blessed Lady, chosen from all eternity by Almighty God to be the mother of His only-begotten Son, was not more highly privileged than all other members of the human race. She is uniquely and highly favoured by Almighty God. And you can see a hierarchy of love and affection in the relationships of Jesus Christ, Our Blessed Lord, Who is very God Himself. Plainly St John was more beloved than the other Apostles, and three of the Apostles —Peter, James and John himself — had a closer relationship to Him than the other nine. Furthermore, those twelve were closer to Him than the disciples.
>
> The infinite variety in our relationships to Almighty God does not imply that any of us is a 'second-class citizen'. Each of us has a unique relationship to Almighty God. The very first step in the spiritual life is to accept that special relationship and to appreciate that no one else has the vocation that we have. No one else can fulfil our vocation for us. We run counter to God's plan in seeking a vocation other than our own, even though that vocation may be objectively a higher one. It is our own vocation that we have to fulfil.[14]

Alfred said himself that none of the book was original. As he saw it he was restating in his own style, with a collage, as it were, of quotations, 'the Faith once delivered to the saints.' If his statements regarding the 'hierarchy of love and affection' do not find an echo in the breast of many bishops nowadays, it did not prevent some of them from highly commending the work. The *papabile* Cardinal Hume (1923–1999) wrote of it: 'A more comprehensive and reliable catechesis would be hard to find.' At Alfred's ninetieth birthday party the Cardinal revealed that Alfred had been the model for his own priesthood. He also called him 'a great priest'. Cardinal Arinze, the formerly *papabile* Prefect Emeritus of the Congregation for Divine Worship and the Discipline of the Sacraments, wrote, 'Every young priest and seminarian in the English-speaking world would do well to have a copy.' Was this, perhaps, an implicit admission from within the magisterium that all was not well in the seminaries?

When I first requested an interview with Alfred, this superannuated cleric (then 94) struck me as a wonderful candidate for interrogation. As the highest of High Tory critics of liberal humanist democracy, a keen follower of beagles, a stubborn upholder of all-male traditions, as one who had been known to remark from his own observation on visits to Spain that the Spanish seemed very happy living under Franco, as a Christian priest living in a socially exclusive club, and as one enjoying the privilege of continuing to say the old Latin rite of Mass, he seemed, from the general reader's point of view, a fascinating monster of political incorrectness, and therefore very good copy. What other individual could offend at once so many canons of the PC creed?

When I first suggested the interview, I imagined it being completed in one session. I did not expect to be called back by my interviewee at least ten times. The trouble was that Alfred would chat on, such that stopping the flow to get him to answer my questions was, as he laughingly admitted, very difficult. And when he started answering them, his replies were often much more fulsome than expected. But I did not want to cut short the considered responses of a man of such holiness, wisdom, experience and wit, nor did I presume to dictate to one so revered. And he kept on inviting me back.

It was not always easy to understand what Alfred said, not from any lack of clarity in his answers, but partly because he spoke in the rapid near-mumble typical of the Edwardian upper class, sounding like a less clear version of Lord Louis Mountbatten, partly because he had always spoken somewhat fuzzily. He told me that when he was a boy his father complained he could not understand a word he said — as did my father when I reintroduced them after a gap of some 30 years! So I had to spend a while replaying my tapes of the interview many times over in order to decipher Alfred's words. It is ironic that someone with such distinct beliefs should have been so indistinct in speech. I abandoned him as a confessor simply because I could not always make out his advice in the box. His friend John Patten says that some people described Alfred's manner of speech '(not unkindly) … as approximating to Serbo-Croat murmured through a damp blanket.'[15]

As to the content of the interview, anyone reading *We Believe*, whatever they think of the teaching expressed, cannot fail to be impressed by the quietly passionate certitude of the author's indestructible faith. It shines out like a dazzling sun from every page. Nonetheless, his very certitude may well beg certain questions in minds more prone to doubt. It was partly to answer some of these potential questions that I interrogated him. In some cases the reader may think that the answer fails to address the question with sufficient precision. I think this is because Alfred believed that, as St John Henry Newman put it 'ten thousand difficulties do not make one doubt.'[16] Thus a restatement in slightly altered form of the point made in print, or a direction to read another passage from *We Believe* is what is frequently given.

It is also true, as he readily acknowledged, that Alfred was fond of digression. The text has been pruned of much of this. In the end, remembering Dom Christopher's account of his instruction by Alfred as an undergraduate in the early 1950s involving three young men sitting together while their chaplain read out the questions and answers of the Catechism and expounded them, allowing no questions, I would sum up his approach to every question thus: 'I have done my best to tell you the Truth which the Church exists to proclaim. Now, on her authority, you must ponder it, and pray for light.' Alfred, like Almighty God, would never have done anything so ungentle as to pressurise or proselytise anyone. He respected, as God does, each person's free will.

> If we have decided that we must belong to the Church because we have recognised her claim to be Christ's revelation to mankind and to be the pillar and ground of truth (1 Timothy 3:15), then it follows that she must be incapable of leading us into error. In other words, she must be infallible or inerrant. The choice of word is not important as long as we understand that if there is a visible body here on earth, the Church, to which we have decided that we must belong once we have come to see her in the light in which she sees herself, then she cannot impose the acceptance of error on us as a condition of membership.[17]

As he says in his preface: 'The book should be read ruminatively and made the subject of prayer.' It will live, I have no doubt, as a classic of Christian apologetic, keeping its place on the shelves alongside St John Henry Newman's *Apologia*, and St Francis de Sales' *Introduction to the Devout Life*, as long as there are readers of a text which, in the words of Cardinal John O'Connor, Archbishop of New York (1920–2000), is 'like food for those who hunger and water for those who thirst.'

As to the need for such food and water today, around the time of my extended interview-by-stages from the latter half of 1994 to some time in the following spring, I met a 24-year-old Cambridge graduate who told me she had heard of Judas, but wasn't sure 'what he was famous for'. Shocked as he would have been at an upbringing and education that could have allowed her to graduate from his own university in such a state of ignorance about the religion that had formed her country's civilisation, Alfred, I am sure, would have felt only tender compassion for her. I hope that some of those who share her ignorance, or even those whose ignorance is greater still, may be enlightened by this book and spurred on to find out more. As for those who do know what Judas was 'famous' for, I trust they will find spiritual illumination, wise counsel and historical interest in these words. They will, I am certain, also enjoy meeting, or re-encountering, Alfred.

NOTES

1. Charles des Forges in *Alfred Gilbey: A Memoir by Some Friends*, ed. David Watkin (London: Michael Russell Publishing Ltd, 2001), 30.

2. Matthew 7:20.

3. He switched to the Oratory from his original regular appointment at Our Lady of the Assumption, Warwick Street, not long after his move to London.

4. And then how I shall lie through centuries,
   And hear the blessed mutter of the Mass,
   And see God made and eaten all day long,
   And feel the steady candle-flame, and taste
   Good strong thick stupefying incense-smoke!
   Robert Browning (1812–89), *The Bishop Orders his Tomb* (1845), ll. 80–84.

5. Monsignor Alfred Gilbey, *We Believe: A Simple Commentary on The Catechism of Christian Doctrine approved by the Archbishops and Bishops of England and Wales* (Leominster, Herefordshire: Gracewing, 2011), (Charlotte, NC: TAN Books, 2013), chapter 8: 'The Visible Church', 99.

6. 'He used to say [like Alfred, only the old rite] Mass in a way that severely annoyed many Tridentinist purists, not least because it took two hours. He celebrated the liturgy with eyes tight shut, knowing the words off by heart. He would move to the right-hand side of the altar with the chalice where his server would proffer the wine and water, eyes closed until he bumped into the server. On one famous occasion the server had seen Fr Charles-Roux go into ecstasy, and momentarily crept off. The result was that Fr Charles-Roux, not finding a server to bump into, had fallen down the altar steps.' Fr. Alexander Lucie-Smith, 'Fr Charles-Roux: He loved the Mass, he loved God. May he now enjoy the vision of God forever', *Catholic Herald* (August 11, 2014).

'"When the New Mass came in I tried it in English, French, Italian, even in Latin—but it was like a children's game," he told me [Cf. The Prayer Book Rebellion of 1549, when the parishioners of Sampford Courtenay in Devon compelled their priest to revert to the old Mass (the Sarum rite). The rebels argued that the new English liturgy was "but lyke a Christmas game."] "So I wrote to Pope Paul, whom I had known when he was Cardinal Montini, and said, 'Holy Father, either you let me celebrate the Old Mass or I leave the priesthood and marry the first pretty girl I meet.'" ... As Fr Charles-Roux's voice dropped to the "blessed mutter" of the silent canon, he seemed to enter an ecstatic trance; it was as if he was blinded by the glory of the Host, which remained elevated

Preface xlv

for an eternity.' Damian Thompson, 'Jean-Marie Charles-Roux, a good and holy priest,' *The Spectator*, (August 8, 2014). Cf. St Philip Neri.

I also remember his look of blissful, overwhelmed ecstasy as he very slowly celebrated the Holy Sacrifice, as well as his cheerfully conspiratorial advice to me to 'steal' a booklet from the stand if I didn't have the cash for it.

7. Gilbey, *We Believe*, Chapter 8, 90.

8. Peter Gregory-Jones in *Alfred Gilbey: A Memoir by Some Friends*, 42.

9. The phrase 'religious dandyism' occurs in Maurice Cowling, *Religion & Public Doctrine in Modern England*, Vol. 1 (Cambridge: Cambridge University Press, 1980). Cf. 'Faced with an arising mass culture that implies vulgarity and a decline in beauty and taste, the dandy acts as a reactionary, desiring the preservation of the grandeur and style of pre-democratic societies.' Melanie Grundmann, *On Dandyism*, Engelsberg Ideas, January 5, 2021, https://engelsbergideas.com/essays/decadence-and-dandyism/.

10. I can't help wondering if she was the woman mentioned in *We Believe* who said to the weary priest instructing her: 'Surely you don't expect me to believe that!', only to get the answer: 'Madam, I don't expect you to believe *anything*. I am merely telling you what the Church teaches.'

11. *We Believe*, Chapter 1, 'The Foundation of Faith in Reason', 18.

12. Alfred was Grand Cross Conventual Chaplain *ad honorem* (the highest rank of chaplain) to the British branch of the Knights of Malta. He had been a member of the Order since 1947. The knights are members of the oldest order of chivalry in the world. Founded in 1099 to guard the pilgrimage route to Jerusalem against the Turks, their primary duty is to serve Christ in the sick poor. This is mainly done through an annual pilgrimage to Lourdes, on which the Knights help to care for the sick. The Order also supports the outstanding Holy Family Hospital in Bethlehem and many other charitable projects.

13. 'When in January 1964 the Bishop of Brentwood invested the Chaplain with the rank of Protonotary Apostolic, it was not only in Papal recognition of his successful defence of Fisher House [which had been threatened with demolition by Cambridge City Council], but as just reward for the large numbers of converts whom he had instructed and received, and the priestly vocations he had helped to foster. During his time as Chaplain from 1932 to 1965, Gilbey instructed some 170 undergraduates in the Faith.' Peter Gregory-Jones, *A History of the Cambridge Catholic Chaplaincy 1895–1965* (Cagliari, Societa Poligrafica Sarda, 1986). Over his 33 years at Cambridge, this averages out at just over five a year—about one new Catholic every month of term, given the six months per year of term-time. Cf: 'He has had more effect on the growth of the Church

in these islands than any other priest in his lifetime. More than eighty priests are priests today because they were received into the Church by Alfred Gilbey. His excellent course of instruction on the Catholic Faith, *We Believe*, is still making converts to this day.' Christopher Monckton of Brenchley, Obituary commemoration, *Catholic Herald* (April 3, 1998).

14. *We Believe*, Chapter 21, 'The Seventh, Tenth and Eighth Commandments', 231–232. Cf. '412. On what is human equality based? All persons enjoy equal dignity and fundamental rights insofar as they are created in the image of the one God, are endowed with the same rational soul, have the same nature and origin, and are called in Christ, the one and only Saviour, to the same divine beatitude.'

'413. How are we to view social inequalities? There are sinful social and economic inequalities which affect millions of human beings. These inequalities are in open contradiction to the Gospel and are contrary to justice, to the dignity of persons, and to peace. There are, however, differences among people caused by various factors which enter into the plan of God. Indeed, God wills that each might receive what he or she needs from others and that those endowed with particular talents should share them with others. Such differences encourage and often oblige people to the practice of generosity, kindness and the sharing of goods. They also foster the mutual enrichment of cultures.'

'414. How is human solidarity manifested? Solidarity, which springs from human and Christian brotherhood, is manifested in the first place by the just distribution of goods, by a fair remuneration for work and by zeal for a more just social order. The *virtue* of solidarity also practices the sharing of the spiritual goods of faith, which is even more important than sharing material goods.' *The Compendium of the Catechism of the Catholic Church* (London: The Incorporated Catholic Truth Society, 2006) 124.

15. John Patten in *Alfred Gilbey: A Memoir by Some Friends*, 112.

16. 'Ten thousand difficulties do not make one doubt, as I understand the subject; difficulty and doubt are incommensurate. There of course may be difficulties in the evidence; but I am speaking of difficulties intrinsic to the doctrines themselves, or to their relations with each other. A man may be annoyed that he cannot work out a mathematical problem, of which the answer is or is not given to him, without doubting that it admits of an answer, or that a certain particular answer is the true one. Of all points of faith, the being of a God is, to my own apprehension, encompassed with most difficulty, and yet borne in upon our minds with most power.' St John Henry Newman, 'Position of my Mind Since 1845', in *Apologia pro Vita Sua* (London: New York: Sheed & Ward, 1976, 160).

17. Gilbey, *We Believe*, Chapter 8, 'The Visible Church', 94.

The Final Interview

THE INTERVIEW
An Introduction

THE FREQUENCY WITH WHICH ALFRED'S characteristic gentle chuckle punctuated his words—often when making the most solemn and serious points—is impossible to capture in cold print. I have remarked it where it bubbles up. The reader may think my use of italics and of the bold key excessive. This is an attempt to echo the *piano* and the **forte** of Alfred's vocal emphases. He used passionate verbal underscoring to give a powerful intensity to many of his utterances. So quietly forceful was he that at times he seemed to drive his words home like nails. Often too, his playful sense of the absurdity of his opponents' positions would rouse him to incredulous fantastical mockery, his voice rising to a pitch of gentle ridicule.

All the quotations from *We Believe* are taken from the Gracewing paperback of 2011. For their numerousness and length you have Alfred to thank. Confident that he had done his best to expound the Faith between the covers of his book, he tended to think that his verbal efforts to define it were bound to be inferior. Quoting Ronald Knox, he said more than once: 'Read my books!' My questions are indicated by numbers and bold text, his answers by 'ANG', my supplementary questions or remarks by 'AH'.

When, one day, towards the end of the course of our conversations, he saw me with a big black book containing my transcript, he looked at me on the verge of blushing and said, in a timid pipe: 'Am I really worth all this?' Let the reader judge.

PART I

The Faith

1. Many people describe matters of faith as 'my truth' or 'your truth', rather than '*the* truth'. They think objective truth in matters of faith or philosophy unattainable. Thus the very word is redefined.
How do you define the word 'truth'?

ANG: ... It's not a subjective thing at all. It may all sound very clumsy—I want poetry—but to make up a definition: it is the assertion of a reality outside oneself which one believes corresponds to fact (*Author's note: Cf. [a] 'A judgement is said to be true when it conforms to the external reality', St Thomas Aquinas,* De Veritate, *Q. 1, A. 1–3; [b] 'Truth is the property of being in accord with fact or reality'* Merriam-Webster's Online Dictionary, 2005).

2. No doubt many people could accept that definition of truth. But they might well protest that the Catholic understanding of objective truth, as expressed in the teachings of the Church, is too rigid and dogmatic. They may even think it distorts the truth by limiting it to the verbal formulae of credal definition.
How can you convince them, as St John Henry Newman was convinced from the age of fifteen, that dogma is 'the fundamental principle of my religion'?[1]

ANG: It has, of course to be precise, to be of any use to anyone. If it's going to be a philosophy of life to be followed, the first things you want are clarity and precision in its enunciation. Men won't follow a will'-o'-the-wisp, a guess at truth. No. They want an assurance. That is part of the universal mystery of the present time: that everyone wants—and must have—the assurance of objectivity. But they'll never be given it. Everything is subjective. Everything has to be undefined. But a definition, it's the first thing a man wants. It's absolutely basic. Definition is at once what people want and what they don't want. But if you provide them with a definition they feel somehow deprived of freedom.

Yes, in those two questions you've really said everything. It's so curious, you see, that people who do want definition, shall we say, in scientific knowledge, *don't* want it in religious knowledge. They certainly want it in scientific knowledge. They can't leave every discussion open-ended! It's either true or it's not true! That, though, is where Euclid is so immensely important, but is left out of our education very much now ('geometry' as we used to call it). The whole value of it as an exact discipline is not the conclusions to which it comes, which are of value to very few people, unless they're jobbing carpenters, but the fact that you can reach *absolutely certain*, inescapable conclusions by a purely intellectual process. An obvious one: Pythagoras' rule for the right-angled triangle: 'The square on the hypotenuse is equal to the sum of the squares on the other two sides.' It's absolutely true. You can't get away from it! It *is* true, and all science is founded on that sort of truth. It isn't a guess, an inspired guess. It does happen to be ever-so inescapably *true*.

There's a lot about all this in *We Believe*. Of course I start by making the great distinction between those truths which are attainable by human reason and those which are obtainable only by faith, and the whole opening of *We Believe* sets out our belief that knowledge of Almighty God, and the nature of Almighty God, are entirely obtainable by reason; knowledge of the immortality of the human soul is entirely obtainable by reason, and realisation of the consequent responsibility of individual human beings is entirely obtainable by reason. All that is a prolegomenon of faith, a foundation.

Only when you've done that—and that's an entirely rational process, we believe—you've then got to consider whether this God has revealed more about Himself than our reason will take us to, and then you come to the *quite, quite, quite* different plane of *revelation*.

The subject of revelation is not attainable by reason *at all*. No amount of human reason is going to take me to a knowledge of the Trinity. No amount of reason is going to take me to a knowledge of the Fall of Man. No amount of human reason's going to take

The Faith

me to a belief in the second person of the Trinity becoming man in order to redeem man from the consequences of the Fall. *None* of those things are attainable by reason. They come to us because God has revealed them. We can see they're *compatible* with reason, but they're not the fruits of reason.

3. Do you think that our human reason, once it accepts the truths it can reach unaided, as outlined in the first chapter of *We Believe* (the existence of Almighty God; His nature; the immortality of the human soul, and our consequent responsibility), and once it sees them as logically inevitable, objective, and therefore unalterable, is better prepared to accept as objective and unalterable the dogmas of the Church?

ANG: Yes, to *accept*, but never to discover or to find. They're not the fruit of human ratiocination at all. The whole of St Thomas Aquinas, the whole works of the scholastics, are not seeking to *attain* those truths; they're seeking to *expound* them, and show their compatibility with human reason. They're not discovering them.

And further, as you've got that point, you're clear that a Christian, having laid the foundations of reason, *starts from the data.* I state that very very clearly in *We Believe*: that theology's *quite quite quite* different from every other intellectual discipline. In all other intellectual disciplines you are seeking to assist your science all you like by constantly trying to push back and increase your knowledge, so gaining further knowledge. With theology, *no*. We're given data, and we can think about that data for all eternity. We can't increase it! So it's no good using reason to dissect this art. We can see more and more in it. That's all that Catholic theology is. So when people say to us, as they very frequently do: 'Oh, you're just indoctrinating the child!', I say: 'That's exactly what I am doing. I *am* trying to indoctrinate the child.' But nowadays that's thought to be politically incorrect.

AH: Of course, the word 'indoctrination' is currently most often used to describe the methods of Communists or Nazis.

ANG: (*Chortling, then with cheerful irony*): Well, Roman Catholicism is very like that! But we *do* believe in indoctrination. The child's got nothing. And of course, we apply it without question to social and natural values. But people will try to take this absurd line: 'You mustn't indoctrinate!' So I say: 'I couldn't agree with you more, but of course, I carry it a bit further than you, you know. We have no business to indoctrinate children to be good members of this country, loyal subjects of the Queen, whatever you like, no business at all! Your boy may want to be Japanese or American when he's eighteen. You've got no earthly business to tell him to be a good Englishman!'

'Well, that's quite different!' Not at all. It's exactly the same thing! You think that those are values of such importance that you teach them to a child. So when people ridicule the idea of teaching a child: 'God is the supreme Spirit, who alone exists of Himself, and is infinite in all perfections',[2] so that the child, almost certainly, will not understand this at all when you give it to him and make him learn it by heart, I always say: 'But he has something to *think* about, though never completely to reach, for the rest of his natural life.'

AH: Likewise, he won't understand if he asks his father what he does, and he says 'I work in a bank.'

ANG: Yes, yes, yes, yes!

AH: But there's no reason not to tell him.

ANG: No. He's got a fact that he can think about, and it has to have *some purpose*.

You can't go through a proposition in Euclid accepting every single step of the argument without reaching the conclusion. You're there before you've got to it. You can't *reject* it. It's inescapable. There's no parallel when it comes to revelation, which you *are* free to accept or to reject. Your mind is *not* compelled, and *that is why faith is a virtue*. Following your reason is not a virtue. It's inescapable. You may be virtuous because of the use you've made of your mental powers, but coming to the conclusion to which your human powers take you is not a virtue at all. You can't do otherwise. Whereas, coming to believe in the divinity of Jesus Christ is something you're not intellectually compelled to do, though you may have many many *suasions*, many *experiences* that

The Faith

lead you that way. But at the end of it all it's an act of virtue to say: 'Thou art the Christ, the Son of the living God', as St Peter did (Matthew 16:16).

No amount of miracles such as He wrought *proved* that He was God. I have got a whole passage on this. They don't prove it in the Euclidean sense. They may be *overwhelming* suasions—if you'd been standing by Our Blessed Lord as He called Lazarus out of the tomb, and out he came—but that didn't *prove*, in the Euclidean sense, that He was God. Here is the divine power at work. But it isn't an intellectual concept.

AH: If He'd proved it, it would mean you had no choice.

ANG: Yes.

AH: Your free will would not be able to operate.

ANG: Yes, exactly. And all this is worked out at considerable length here:

The very nature of a gift involves a free act of the will; and so it is with Faith: it needs to be freely offered by Almighty God. Certainly it needs to be freely accepted by the individual. It cannot be forced.

And there you see the need for more than an act of the intellect.[3]

4. Many people who never open a Bible will agree more readily with the statement 'Verily, thou art a God that hidest thyself' (Isaiah 45:15) than with any of the more positive affirmations of God's existence contained within its covers. They may well agree also with the Logical Positivist philosopher A.J. Ayer, who said in response to the statement that God was present in his room even though he couldn't see Him: 'Well, for all I know, there may be a hippopotamus in my room as well, and I can't see that either!'[4]

How can this objection be met, for those who have had no religious experience?

ANG: The Apostles are great comforts to me. I think: 'Gor! How slow they were!' So it seems to us, harking back. But Our Blessed Lord revealed Himself very, very, very gradually, so that even after the Resurrection they didn't believe. They had to wait till Pentecost.

AH: And they appear to have thought that He was going to be a military leader.

ANG: Oh yes indeed, yes — asked for places in His kingdom and so on. And on top of it, the mother of James asked if her son should sit at His right hand or His left when He came to receive His own. It's *extraordinary* how obtuse they were! No it isn't! Because what they had to believe in was something much much much beyond human reason.

> Now, the distinction between the content of something revealed and the credibility of the revealer is something which we are always making in ordinary life. We continually believe things because other people tell us them. In the case of ordinary life many of these things can be checked by us. But I want for a moment to emphasise how constantly, in the ordinary conduct of our life, we are believing things because we are told them. I want to emphasise it, too, because we ought not to make heavy weather about doing in our relationship with Almighty God what we do daily in our dealings with other people.
>
> Take an immediate example: why do I believe everything I do believe about you? It is precisely because you have told me. Why do I believe your name? I could, of course, check it. I could ring up and ask for confirmation, or ask to see your birth certificate. But that is not why I believe it. I believe it because of your credibility.
>
> Take another example: if a distinguished professor were to tell me something about his proper line of study, which is a completely closed book to me, so that I could not check it at all, I would believe what he told me because he was known to be a truthful and reliable person.
>
> I stress these points because in the revelation of Almighty God the actual content of what He is revealing to us is beyond our power even to check or, in the case of the mysteries, to understand. We are accepting what has been revealed because we believe it to have been revealed by Almighty God and because we know Him to be the very truth. We believe His revelation, therefore, through faith.[5]

The Faith

We had entrance examinations in my first term at Trinity in 1920, and in one of them there were optional papers, one of which, *incredible* now, was to study Paley's *Evidences for Christianity*.[6] Actually, it's a great work. Cardinal Manning said: 'I read pages 15 to 16 and the argument has never left me', or words to that effect. One dilemma Paley puts in the way of the sceptic about the Divinity of Our Blessed Lord is to say that first of all He certainly claimed to be God, and certainly a man, and that there are only three possibilities. Either: He was a lunatic claiming to be God. People who claim to be God are put in lunatic asylums. Or He was a deceiver, claiming to be God but knowing perfectly well that He wasn't — so that the greatest moral force the world has ever known was a prodigal crook! Or you are left with the third possibility: that He was who He claimed to be.

5. If they have accepted your arguments, the inquirer now understands that truth must be objective, and that dogmatic definition is a logical necessity, enabling the Church to expound her beliefs with precision. Their next question is a perennial conundrum:
How can a loving God have allowed the cruelties of which the twentieth century bears the most appalling record?

ANG: It ought to be true that the world is delightful — as we believe it was before the Fall — but the Fall has had these appalling consequences, not only in human nature and its wickedness, but also in the inanimate world. We can't imagine what it was like before, but certainly there are many things that have arisen here that destroy happiness: death, of course, and serious disease. They're all the consequences of the Fall. But the doctrine that people most completely reject *is* the Fall of Man.[7]

It doesn't make any sense at all. But how people can believe that, who read — or glance at — their newspaper every day and see *horror after horror after horror*! Oh, just in this morning's paper: a man breaking into a policeman's house, throwing petrol over everything, putting a match to it, then bolting out, leaving him to die from his burns. Absolutely pointless. And they think, so to speak, he probably got 'the wrong man'.

All this terrible crime today! But you know *if you look into your own heart, you can know there's no crime to which you would not sink. No. None!* We all of us have frightful impulses, of vice and violence and everything, and beastliness and callousness towards other people's suffering. We're all horrible creatures really. I always pray: 'There but for the grace of God go I.'[8]

6. There are two kinds of horrors in the world, though, those caused directly by human agency, and those like the recent earthquake in Russia that killed 2,000 people.
How do you explain or justify that as an act of God?

ANG: It never stops, does it? If it isn't an earthquake in Russia, it's going to the hospital, if you like. Have you ever been to Lourdes? ... One sees such a concatenation of human suffering there. Appalling! So so *edifying. Wonderful* that people with frightful sicknesses are carried for miles and miles of appalling discomfort so as to visit Lourdes, hoping for a cure, but it's so seldom vouchsafed. But the *blinding*—or the visible—faith and acceptance! Oh, it's wonderful!

I always come back from Lourdes thinking I shall *never never* complain again. But I do! We all do. Well, 'there but for the grace of God go I', complaining again!

7. Are you saying that natural disasters, disease, hereditary deformities and the like are all symptoms of Original Sin?

ANG: Yes. They're consequences of the Fall, certainly, all the disorders in the world, as in our own selves.

AH: As Milton puts it, describing the effect on nature as Eve bites into the forbidden fruit:

> Earth felt the wound, and Nature from her seat
> Sighing through all her works gave signs of woe
> That all was lost.[9]

In Milton's inspiration, Genesis 3:17, God says to Adam: 'Cursed is the ground because of you.' That makes God sound very frightening.

The Faith 13

ANG: The frightening thing, of course, is having given us free will. That's one of the most staggering mysteries, really. There are those who think He should have made us automata, if He wanted to create us at all, and pull the wires Himself. But no. He's given us free will, and we *are* able, as our first parents were, to choose evil.

8. We have many 'great teachers' to choose from, who have left their spiritual legacies in various parts of the world: Mohammed, the Buddha, Guru Nanak (the founder of Sikhism), etc. Why should we have to choose Christ and reject the rest?

ANG: We must start by looking at those statements. There's only one of them that can be true. They aren't all reconcilable with each other. Then, given that these human leaders who had been thinking out these thoughts for a long time and reached five or six powerful conclusions which are fairly widespread, you're still faced with the fact that they're mutually exclusive.

I say in *We Believe* that, of all the great religious teachers of the world, Christ is the only one who has *achieved* something. The others may have a very high moral doctrine, if you like, exemplary lives, but He is the only one of Whom it's claimed, as He Himself claimed, to have changed the whole relationship between God and man *by an act*. He changed the whole thing by something He did: saved us from certain Hell and opened the way to Heaven. Whatever else may be said for any of the others, none of them did that.

9. What is the point of God taking human flesh, and why did He have to be crucified?

ANG: Jesus Christ was able to suffer and to die — *God knows what suffering!* — as you and I are, as a man. He was a man, and so able to shoulder, in his humanity, the burden of the sinfulness of the world — ah! But able to endow that suffering with an *infinite* value — because He was also God. That's why the Incarnation's absolutely central to what we believe. It's all in my chapter on the Incarnation: how if you emphasise one concept at the expense of the other you destroy the whole point of Christ's suffering and death.[10] If you think He was only a man who suffered and died, or that He was only God, allowing this redemption of infinite value, that allows alternate concepts to take over. No. He was one *single* man. Not two men: two natures.

One of the most moving [*overwhelmed, near tears*] ... the Mass is a *wonderful wonderful* thing! I set it out years ago in my speech on my fiftieth anniversary of ordination, how most things in life lose their awe and majesty and wonder by constant repetition. Not so the priesthood [*long pause*].

Never, never can one celebrate Mass without *awe* and wonder!

AH: Though people try to!

ANG: They try to make out: 'Oh, it's a jolly family meal', yes. But when you turn around to see the people waiting for the *Ecce Agnus Dei! Ecce qui tollit peccata mundi!*...[11]

It can get hold of that awful burden weighing on us all, and can expiate it, this wafer of bread. What is covered? We can't see Him: Incarnate God; very God Himself clothed in human flesh; not just clothed in it either, but *being very God*, the God begotten, not made.

We feed on this incredible mystery: that one single person, *one single person*, has together two natures, both human and divine, and therefore is able to shoulder all the ills of mankind. That's the root of everything. I say this repeatedly. And that is the *central* mystery of all we believe: the Incarnation. All the other mysteries are seen in their right perspective as preparatory to, or flowing out of, this central mystery.

10. There are very many Christian denominations. How can I be sure that the Catholic Church is the one true Church founded by Christ?

ANG: They can't be synthesised, because they're contradictory, all the different presentations ... My little book will answer your questions far better than I can spontaneously:

> What I want you to consider now is this: that this mystical body, whereby we are incorporated into Christ, and form one body with Him, is itself incarnate or embodied in a visible institution here on earth. The Catholic

Church is not an invisible body any more than the Incarnation was an invisible presence. At the Incarnation the Word, the Second Person of the Blessed Trinity, was conceived in the womb of Our Blessed Lady, was born by her and came into the world as a visible material man like you and me, having height, weight, displacement, and the rest. He was not a spirit pure and simple: He was really and truly a man. And we believe that that Incarnation of Christ continues in the Church, so that she is not an invisible and disincarnate entity. We believe, therefore, in what is called the visible unity of the Church.

Now, though it is very seldom emphasised, that really is the dividing line between ourselves and all other Christians, certainly in the West.[12] You may deny or disagree with that statement; but come to consider it yourself and ask yourself what other body of professing Christians claims to be the Church, as the Catholic Church does. As you know, they all say, in the Apostles' Creed, 'I believe in the Catholic Church,' but if you press them you will always find that they are professing belief in an invisible entity. When they say they believe in the Catholic Church they may mean that they believe in the unity of all those in a state of grace, the oneness of all true believers or a hundred and one other things, but never do they identify the Catholic Church with a single, visible organised body here on earth. Dr William Temple, Archbishop of Canterbury, used to say, 'I believe in the Holy Catholic Church, and sincerely regret that it does not at present exist.'

The error underlying this remark is, despite all superficial differences, precisely the same as that of the Reformers of the sixteenth century when they appealed to the primitive Church. Both are effectively saying that in the here and now Christ's promises have failed. But the here and now is the only time I have, in which, with God's grace, to work out my salvation. In that task the ideal Church whether of the past or of the future is powerless to help me.[13]

NOTES

1. 'From the age of fifteen, dogma has been the fundamental principle of my religion: I know no other religion; I cannot enter into the idea of any other sort of religion; religion, as a mere sentiment, is to me a dream and a mockery. As well can there be filial love without the fact of a father, as devotion without the fact of a Supreme Being.' (St John Henry Newman, 'History of my Religious Opinions from 1833 to 1839', in *Apologia pro Vita Sua*, 32–33.)

2. Alfred quotes the answer to question 17: What is God? in *The Catechism of Christian Doctrine approved by the Archbishops and Bishops of England and Wales* (London: The Incorporated Catholic Truth Society, 1971). Known to generations of Catholics as 'the Penny Catechism', due to its cost in days gone by.

3. Gilbey, *We Believe*, chapter 2, 'Divine Revelation', 27.

4. I cannot trace the hippopotamus quote from Ayer. I cited it from memory, from an interview I saw on television many years ago. Even if not authentic, it expresses Ayer's contempt for 'metaphysics'. Ayer (1910–1989) was an English philosopher known for his promotion of logical positivism, particularly in his books *Language, Truth and Logic* (1936) and *The Problem of Knowledge* (1956).

5. Gilbey, *We Believe*, chapter 2, 'Divine Revelation', 26. Cf. 'And what I wish you particularly to observe, is that we continually trust our memory and our reasoning powers in this way, though *they often deceive us*. This is worth observing, because it is sometimes said we cannot be *certain* that our faith in religion is not a mistake. I say our memory and reason often deceive us; yet no one says it is therefore absurd and irrational to continue to trust them; and for this plain reason, because *on the whole* they are true and faithful witnesses, because it is only *at times* that they mislead us; so that the chance is, that they are right in this case or that, which happens to be before us; and (again) because in all practical matters we are obliged to dwell upon not what *may be possibly*, but what is *likely* to be. In matters of daily life, we have no time for fastidious and perverse fancies about the minute chances of our being deceived. We are obliged to act at once, or we should cease to live. There is a chance (it cannot be denied) that our food today may be poisonous—we cannot be quite certain—but it looks the same and tastes the same, and we have good friends round us; so we do not abstain from it, for all this chance, though it is real. This necessity of acting promptly is our happiness in this world's matters; in the concerns of a future life, alas! we have time for carnal and restless thoughts about possibilities. And this is our *trial*;

The Faith 17

and it will be our condemnation, if with the experience of the folly of such idle fancyings about what may be, in matters of this life, we yet indulge them as regards the future. If it be said, that we sometimes do distrust our reasoning powers, for instance, when they lead us to some unexpected conclusion, or again our memory, when another's memory contradicts it, this only shows that there *are* things which we should be weak or hasty in believing; which is quite true. Doubtless there is such a fault as credulity, or believing too readily and too much (and this, in religion, we call superstition); but this neither shows that *all* trust is irrational, nor again that trust is necessarily irrational, which is founded on what is but likely to be, and may be denied without an actual absurdity. Indeed, when we come to examine the subject, it will be found that, strictly speaking, we know little more than that we exist, and that there is an Unseen Power whom we are bound to obey. Beyond this we must *trust*; and first our senses, memory, and reasoning powers; then other authorities: — so that, in fact, almost all we do, every day of our lives, is on trust, i.e., *faith*.' (St John Henry Newman, *Parochial and Plain Sermons*, Sermon 15: Religious Faith Rational, preached on May 24, 1829. Source: https://www.newmanreader.org/works/parochial/volume1/sermon15.html).

6. Alfred went up to Trinity College, Cambridge in October 1920. George V had been on the throne for ten years. The nation was still coming to terms with the terrible losses of the Great War. Lloyd George continued as Prime Minister of the wartime Coalition government. In Ireland in March, a magistrate dragged from a train and killed had become the twenty-ninth victim of political murder in that country that year. That same October, several things were to happen which the young Alfred might have seen as ominous signs for the future: on 7th, the first 100 women were admitted to Oxford to take full university degrees, of an equal status with those of the male undergraduates; on 16th, the coal miners went on strike; on 28th, the suffragette leader Sylvia Pankhurst was imprisoned for six months after urging people to loot the docks. Only two years earlier, the Representation of the People Act had given men over twenty-one and women over thirty who were householders the right to vote (women over twenty-one were not to get the vote until 1928). Source: Rodney Castleden, *British History* (London: Parragon Book Service Ltd, 1994).

7. 'To consider the world in its length and breadth, its various history, the many races of man, their starts, their fortunes, their mutual alienation, their conflicts… their aimless courses… the greatness and littleness of man, his far-reaching aims, his short duration… the disappointments of life, the defeat of good, the success of evil, physical pain, mental anguish,

the prevalence and intensity of sin, the pervading idolatries, the corruptions, the dreary hopeless irreligion, that condition of the whole race, so fearfully yet exactly described in the Apostle's words, "having no hope and without God in the world," — all this is a vision to dizzy and appal; and inflicts on the mind a profound mystery, which is absolutely beyond human solution.'

'What shall be said to this heart-piercing, reason-bewildering fact? I can only answer, that either there is no Creator, or this living society of men is in a true sense discarded from His presence… *if* there be a God, *since* there is a God, the human race is implicated in some terrible aboriginal calamity. It is out of joint with the purpose of its Creator. This is a fact, a fact as true as the fact of its existence; and thus the doctrine of what is theologically called original sin becomes to me almost as certain as that the world exists, and as the existence of God.' (St John Henry Newman, *Apologia pro Vita Sua*, 162–163).

8. Ironically, this constant prayer of Alfred's is also attributed to one John Bradford (c. 1510–55), an English Protestant martyr burned at the stake in the reign of Mary Tudor (1553–58). On seeing a group of criminals being led to their execution, he exclaimed: 'But for the grace of God there goes John Bradford.' Source: Elizabeth Knowles, ed., *Oxford Dictionary of Quotations*, 6th Edition (Oxford: Oxford University Press 2004).

9. John Milton, *Paradise Lost*, Book IX, ll. 782–784.

10. Gilbey, *We Believe*, Chapter 4, 'Jesus Christ, God Incarnate', 51–58.

11. Alfred is quoting the Tridentine Roman Missal, containing the Order of Mass as established by the Council of Trent (1543–63, promulgated 1570, revised 1962). The Latin means: 'Behold the Lamb of God: behold Him Who takes away the sins of the world!'

12. The little phrase 'certainly in the West' is a necessary qualification: the Orthodox Church, whose orders and sacraments Rome respects as valid, also claims an unbroken apostolic link with the Church founded by Christ. It is closer to Rome in doctrine than all other churches but has broken its formal link with the Apostolic See.

13. Gilbey, *We Believe*, Chapter 8, 'The Visible Church', 89–90.

PART 2

Controversies

1. Why He Resigned

Throughout your time as the longest-serving Chaplain to the (male) Catholic undergraduates of Cambridge University [1932–65], women were forbidden to attend Mass at Fisher House [the chaplaincy building], or to make use of it socially. In this you were at one with the famous Bible translator and brief contemporary of yours in the same office at Oxford, Mgr Ronald Knox [in post 1926–39]. Nonetheless, there were people who questioned this traditional policy as far back as the 1930s. In response to such a questioner, in a 1937 letter about female 'students' (not, then, undergraduates, for women were not to attain equal status with men at Cambridge until ten years later), you wrote:

> I must confess that though I am most desirous that the spiritual welfare of these students should be secured, I cannot see that their cure could be combined with that of the Catholic undergraduates without serious detriment to the work of the chaplaincy.[1]

You added that Cambridge was a special case compared to 'modern universities' because of its 'more marked' gulf between the sexes. In 1937, of course, both the university and society were very different from today, but you maintained this line unwaveringly right up to 1965, when you resigned after a meeting of the Fisher Society [*the chaplaincy committee of undergraduates*], backed by the dons of the Cambridge University Catholic Association, had been deliberately called in your absence by members determined to force through the admission of women.

In what ways did you think the admission of women would have caused 'serious detriment' to your work?

ANG: Have you been following the controversy at the Oxford and Cambridge Club? It rests on an entire illusion, of course. Well, first of all, it's blackmail, trying to force the committee to admit women to full membership. And the critics take their stand on this entirely unfounded idea that because membership of the Oxford and Cambridge Club is *confined* to male undergraduates of both universities, therefore—a complete *non sequitur*—everyone who has *been* to either of the ancient universities has a right to be a member of the club. Well, of course that's nonsense.[2]

A club is a purely voluntary organisation. The membership of it is controlled by those who are already members, and they can choose whom they *like* to join it. No one has a *right* to be a member of the Oxford and Cambridge—come to think of it, not even the members. They've no *right* to be there. It's a perfectly free institution that *elects* to its membership whomever it chooses to elect, and has until now chosen to elect only men.

But now it's always talked about as to how *invidious* it is that women are *forbidden* to use the grand staircase, are *forbidden* to use the library, as though it's a punitive infliction on them! [*With an exasperated chuckle*]: They *just aren't there!*

Well now, the position of the Catholic Chaplain was in *this* respect exactly the same. *When* I was appointed Chaplain to the Catholics at the University of Cambridge, *no women were members of the* **university**.[3] Women generally, taking their stand upon the sword-strokes of Equality, have been trying to get into the ancient universities for 100 years, and have now at last succeeded in getting in, not only to the universities but to individual colleges. They've achieved what they'd been aiming at for years. But they had no *right* to it. They have been conducting a campaign which has produced the fruits which they wanted. They weren't *penalised*. They weren't *forbidden* to go, as if from a position which they had traditionally enjoyed. They just were not admitted! As with the club.

AH: But they *felt* it as a prohibition.

ANG: Well, they felt it, but they were entirely erroneous. You can't feel any feeling of injustice or resentment if a *voluntary* organisation, which no one's *bound* to join, or no one has a *right* to join, an institution that can settle who *does* belong and who *doesn't*, won't admit you.

When I went up as chaplain in '32, the two colleges of Girton and Newnham were very important organisations that were *gunning* to get in, and by degrees were—fatally, of course—given concessions. Once you give a concession, the process starts. It's grandmother's footsteps. But when I went, I made it quite clear that I had no intention of admitting women. And nor had the Chaplain at Oxford. But *then*, Oxford sold a pass.[4]

Once it happened, the public was beginning to see this more and more as a legitimate grievance which should be corrected. A view founded on the entirely erroneous concept of equality: there must be nothing that's not open to everyone. It isn't true. Firstly, as I must have told you, egalitarianism is that philosophy which believes that all men—and I'm using the word 'men' meaning men and women, as it always does—all men are born equal. [*Matter-of-factly*]: Well, that, of course, is balderdash. They're not! It's all part of the entirely erroneous theory that presumes that we come out on a belt, from a sort of producer!

Each individual is an absolutely *unique* creation of Almighty God, with a different tone of individual voice. Our gifts and handicaps, yours and mine, are entirely different. Start at the very beginning. When you're born—which makes, [*grinning broadly*] what, six years between us, or more [there were, in fact, over sixty]? Yes: equality doesn't exist.

In the world Almighty God has created, *every single thing* is a unique creation. Well, *everything* is. Every star differs from every other star. Every leaf on the tree is different from every other leaf. Every pebble on the sand is different from every other pebble.

If that's true of inanimate creation, it's no less true of the animal creation, and most obviously true of man, who is, of all the visible creation, the most nearly the reflection of Almighty God.[5] Everything in creation, right down to you and me sitting here now, is unique, and *not* 'equal'—a cruel word, has no meaning. There's no way in which you and I are equal to one another.

So all this pressure of women entering the ancient universities has finally succeeded in what they've been gunning to do for a very long time. But... going back to my undergraduate days, the very thought would almost have produced a riot. In fact, I could show you some photographs of a sort of riot of 1897, a protest outside the Senate House when the grace for admitting female members was thrown out by the Senate.[6] When that was repeated in my undergraduate days, and feeling was running *very* strong *against*, so much so that there was a terrible row with all the egalitarians, who by then included many of the dons, who were outraged when one particular member of the Senate came out and *announced* to the people waiting outside, the result, and said: 'Now go and take the news to Newnham!'—at which (almost in my first year, I think, at Trinity)[7]—the crowd rushed up to Newnham, where unfortunately they found a lot of builder's posts marking the digging of the road (I can't think what they were doing, making some major alteration)—and two of them were using them as battering-rams for the college gates. Oh, there was a terrible row! They got punished for bad behaviour, and the poor man who went out and said: 'Now go and take the news to Newnham!' got a *frightful* ticking-off from the University!

That's the background. But the pressure's gone on relentlessly, accelerated, of course, by two World Wars which were all on the side of egalitarianism, and finally, they made it. But all colleges continued for a time to hold out. They went down like nine-pins once one of them had gone. But as long as the colleges were still entirely masculine, I said I was appointed *for that*, and it's not for me to—*and nor will I*—admit women to Fisher House, which was intended as a chaplaincy for male members of the University, *because there were no others.*

Ronnie Knox was chaplain at Oxford, and I was Chaplain at Cambridge, and our message was the same as that of many others. Then the War came. First of all, Ronnie Knox left to translate the Bible... and Alfonso de Zulueta, a great friend of mine, who was a parish priest, was appointed Chaplain at Oxford, and the same position continued: he was Chaplain to the men.[8] The men were much more numerous at Oxford. But at both places provision was made for the women. At both there was a nunnery, which was supposed to be the centre for them. But of course *they wanted to be with the men.*

At Oxford it was *awful*. The nunnery at Cherwell Edge was supposed to be their chaplaincy. Ronnie Knox continued to be Chaplain to the men only. Fr Vernon Johnson, a noted convert, was appointed Chaplain to the women.[9] Then Alfonso went to be Chaplain to the men, and he continued the same policy and outlook. But Alfonso was hunted out of Oxford by the Spanish pinks. At Cambridge we got lots of German Jewish refugees. They got a lot of the so-called refugees from Franco at Oxford.[10] And they conducted a campaign to get Alfonso out, saying he was a foreigner, which was technically true, an aristocrat, which was undoubtedly true, and a fascist — which was wholly untrue.

But anyhow, they put great pressure to get him out on the Foreign Office, put pressure on our bishops — who were *craven*, and told Alfonso it was in the general interest he should resign, and he did. But what followed was: Vernon Johnson, who was there looking after the women, was asked to take over the men as well, as a war measure, a temporary war measure, and Alfonso was to go back when peace was declared.

AH: Which never happened.

ANG: Of *course* it never happened. No, nothing ever does. But that is how the change came about at Oxford. But Alfonso, he was a misinterpreted character, but clear in his views.

If it had happened to me, a nasty man like me, I should have brought up this situation and said: 'Peace *has* been declared, and I'm taking the next train to Oxford.' But, no, he gave way, under this pressure. I never did, of course; well, I had no occasion to. But I also arranged for a nunnery at Cambridge to be the women's centre, and so the priests were at least nominally their chaplains. I don't know how much they made use of it, or of them. There were some rather distinguished ones. They went, many of them, strongly for the opinion of the women, and put pressure on — well, tried to put pressure on — me, and I said [*in an exasperated tone*]: 'No, no, no, no. I've been appointed for one thing, which I'm doing, or trying to do, and I won't take pressure from my own flock.' I said: 'If you *want* to put this to the Board, the Board is my authority.[11] If the Board says I must admit women, I just resign. It's perfectly simple.'

Some people continued to put pressure on the Board. So the Board said: 'Are you prepared to admit women?' I said: 'No. If the Board insists on admitting women, I shall resign.' So the Board then [1965] passed a resolution which said *when I retired* it would go. But that really positioned me in an intolerable hole, and so I *did*, well, accept, and said: 'Well, right, I shall go.' I was going in a year or so anyway, but when the pressure on me was insufferable, I said: 'Now I'm allowed to go by the terms of my appointment', and they gave me six months' notice, that's it, and walked out. *That's* the end of it—astonishing![12]

But you must see it always not as an *imposition by me*, as it's thought to be, but a *continuance* by me of what was the position antecedently. So don't say, as people will: 'Oh, women were *forbidden* to go to the chaplaincy!' I kept the chaplaincy *strictly* for those for whom I'd been appointed: for men, and men's colleges. I just carried on, saying: 'This is what I was appointed for; this is what I'm doing; this is what I will continue to do.' And then, I *did* bring in—purely a *practical* argument—well, it goes back to the theoretical argument: men and women are not *equal*. They are designed by Almighty God to be *complementary*, and that is what they are. Read your Old Testament, read what you will. Women are *complementary* to men. They may, if you like, make up one whole: the family is one whole, *yes*. But that they're the same or equal to men *means nothing*. They are *not* men, and men are not women!

Well, if you couldn't take the *theoretical* point, consider the purely practical point: you can *see* that women are made to be complementary to men. You can't combine them in *vastly different numbers*. For argument's sake, let's say the men were 200, and the women 25! There's no *earthly* way of making a whole of 25 women and 200 men. You *kill* the nature of the place as it is. Men's society with men is a quite different thing to mixed society. You kill it at one fell blow without having a *balanced complement*.[13]

It would be impossible to continue as I set out to do. It couldn't be done. And of course the *madness* of egalitarianism has got to the point now that they begin to see the *practical* difficulties. At Cambridge when I went up, no one, as a college freshman—unless they were scholars (scholars had 'rights'!)—was permitted to live in college. They... could do so... in their second or third years... but when this started to be applied to women who had been living with their boyfriends in lodgings, [*in a tone of amused exasperation*]: the boyfriend couldn't understand why he couldn't take the woman with him!

And even now, you can't have double quarters, can you? I mean you can't say: 'Well, I want my girlfriend to share a double set with me'! It'll come, of course.[14] Did you see that recent headline reporting the Anglican bishop who said that living in sin is no sin?[15] It's the same principle all along, isn't it? It's all going on a forced basis: grandmother's footsteps. No one, no don, believes in sin now.

What our labourings show you is how misleading it is to say: 'Old Monsignor Gilbey *forbade* women to come to the Chaplaincy.' Completely worthless. It's a very important concept. You see, it breaks into things like immigration, and are people assimilable to all the cultural differences of our civilisation or not?

Egalitarianism goes round with this *mad* idea that we're all square pegs — or round, as the case may be — and that we can be put from one hole into another. It has had *enormous* political consequences, hasn't it?...

Silly but kind visitors who would come and see me in my later years when I was at Cambridge [1932–65] would often ask: 'Do you find that Cambridge has changed very much since you first knew it?', and I restrained myself from answering: 'Darn silly question!'

2. If you believe that your anxiety about 'serious detriment' to the work of the chaplaincy has been vindicated in the last 30 years, do you think it would help that work today if the present Chaplain at Cambridge were able to revive the old system of two sexually segregated chaplaincies?

ANG: Things have so completely changed that no, no chaplain could take the line I took. In those days the colleges were still monosexual. The vast majority of colleges were still men and men only. And... a great part of the value of Cambridge was *precisely* that degree of cohesion which comes from monosexual society... That's the end of your question, but earlier on, I would say: *because* they are different — which is of course what no one will concede — that is: the sexes *are* different...

We in this country think we have, for all its limitations, a fairly balanced, homogeneous society. The introduction of any number of *different* people from different backgrounds would destroy that, destroy that *very* wonderful homogeneity which we have, and produce a *very* imbalanced society. That's what would have happened to you if you had tried to make a chaplaincy, say, out of 150 or 170 men and suddenly injected into it eight or ten women...[16]

AH: What do you think would have been the practical consequences of admitting women?

ANG: Yes, this is being said, isn't it, in the homosexual debate, where the [armed] services are *still* excluding homosexuals... saying it's a result of their *long* experience... That, of course, should be abolished. It's nonsense. No other country imposes this![17]

Of course, you've seen it in club life perfectly! As soon as you say membership is open to women, you change the whole character of the thing. Men have a *natural* tendency to congregate, and like each other's company, and *women do not!*[18]

I said that to one of my flock and got a letter from a foreign woman saying: 'Well, we do!' But it isn't true, not in the same way. What women really want is a husband! It's as simple as that. Not every man wants a wife, but every woman wants a husband. They want somebody on whom to centre their lives, and they've got a naturally installed tendency. They have a role. They're very conscious of what it is. No doubt about that: wife and mother—and a very elevated and wonderful role it is. There's a whole passage from Maisie Ward's life of Chesterton where he's attacking the concept that the *metier* of life for which women are made is something trivial as the greatest irreverence.

[*He refers me to his collection of favourite quotations,* The Commonplace Book of Monsignor A. N. Gilbey]:

> In the free family there will be a division of the two sides of life, between the man and the woman. The man must be, to a certain extent, a specialist; he must do one thing well enough to earn the daily bread. The woman is the universalist; she must do a hundred things for the safeguarding and development of the home. The modern fad of talking of the narrowness of domesticity especially provoked Chesterton. 'I cannot', he said, 'with the utmost energy of imagination conceive what they mean. When domesticity, for instance, is called drudgery, all the difficulty

arises from a double meaning in the word. If drudgery only means dreadfully hard work, I admit the woman drudges in the home, as a man might drudge at the Cathedral of Amiens, or drudge behind a gun at Trafalgar. But if it means that the hard work is more heavy because it is trifling, colourless and of small import to the soul, then as I say, I give it up; I do not know what the words mean. To be Queen Elizabeth within a definite area, deciding sales, banquets, labours and holidays; to be Whiteley[19] within a certain area, providing toys, boots, sheets, cakes and books; to be Aristotle within a certain area, teaching morals, manners, theology and hygiene; I can understand how this might exhaust the mind, but I cannot imagine how it could narrow it. How can it be a large career to tell other people's children about the Rule of Three, and a small career to tell one's own children about the universe? How can it be broad to be the same thing to everyone, and narrow to be everything to someone? No; a woman's function is laborious, but because it is gigantic, not because it is minute. I will pity Mrs Jones for the hugeness of her task; I will never pity her for its smallness'... [20]

3. In *We Believe* you make the Church's traditional distinction between the Commandments which must be obeyed in order to obtain salvation, and the Counsels, which need only be followed by that minority called to the life of perfection. The distinction is made most strikingly in your consideration of Christ's encounter with the rich young man. You say this is 'a distinction which Our Lord makes'. You cite the passage:

> And behold, one came and said to him: Good Master, what good shall I do that I may have life everlasting? And Jesus said unto him: Why askest thou me concerning good? One is good, God. But if thou wilt enter into life, keep the Commandments. He said to him: Which?
>
> And Jesus said: Thou shalt do no murder, Thou shalt not commit adultery, Thou shalt not steal, Thou shalt not bear false witness. Honour thy father and thy mother, and thou shalt love thy neighbour as thyself.
>
> The young man saith to him: All these have I kept from my youth. What is yet wanting to me?

> Jesus saith to him: If thou wilt be perfect, go, sell what thou hast, and give to the poor and thou shalt have treasure in heaven: and come, follow me. And when the young man heard his word, he went away sad: for he had great possessions. (Matthew 19:16–22; Mark 10:17–22; Luke 18:18–23).

You comment:

> The young man was in the way of salvation through keeping the Commandments. These he could not disregard without sin. The call to the life of perfection, on the other hand, was an invitation which he was morally free to accept or refuse. The Gospels make it clear that, even in Our Blessed Lord's most intimate circles, there were those who followed such a call and those who neither followed nor probably even received it.[21]

But I wonder if the encounter is quite as clear-cut as you claim. You may have read Ronald Knox's story 'The Rich Young Man: A Fantasy', in which the Good Thief crucified next to Christ turns out to have started out as the rich young man. Does this not imply that, in the opinion of this highly learned and authoritative translator of the Bible, the rich young man had in fact missed his vocation to poverty, and so sinned gravely?

After all, if he is 'morally free to accept or refuse' the call to perfection, why does he ask: 'What is yet wanting to me?' And why does he go away 'sad'? And, further, why does Jesus say, immediately after the young man's departure (in slightly differing words, Matthew 19:23–24; Mark 10:23–25; Luke 18:24–25):

> Verily I say unto you, That a rich man shall hardly enter into the kingdom of heaven.
> And again I say unto you, It is easier for a camel to go through the eye of a needle, than for a rich man to enter into the kingdom of God?

ANG: As I've *always said*, we should *all of us, all of us, all of us, always* remember that we are called to lives of sanctity. We should all discover a vocation somewhere. My entire vocation is to priesthood. But every single one of us is *made* by Almighty God: made for a purpose, whether it be life in the world, whether it be a contemplative order, whether it be an active order...we're made for a purpose. And *none of those are mandatory*, whereas the Commandments *are* mandatory. You can't save your immortal soul if you willingly, knowingly, unrepentantly break the Commandments, knowing what you're doing. No: you damn yourself.

This was guyed, you know, by my successor Fr Incledon. He reviewed *We Believe* years ago when it first came out.[22] But people who read that dialogue *always* concertina it. They leave out the passage which comes afterwards in which His disciples ask Our Blessed Lord: 'Who then can be saved?' (Matthew 19:25; Mark 10:26; Luke 18:26), and He does *not* of course answer: 'Only those who sell all that they have and give it to the poor'! No! He says: 'With men this is impossible; but with God all things are possible.' That makes it quite clear...

I'm not complaining. I'm only saying this book has *never been reviewed*. It's had an enormous *number* of reviews, many of them very kindly intentioned, and all so kind about me! But the really knotty problems like this one I have never seen addressed, except disparagingly, by Fr Incledon.

AH: May this interview fill that gap.

ANG: Well, I'm all for it...

AH: But if the young man was really 'morally free to accept or refuse' the call to poverty, why did he go away 'sad'?

ANG: But he's not free to refuse the call to *sanctity*...

AH: ...And then Our Lord says: 'It is easier for a camel to go through the eye of a needle, than for a rich man to enter into the kingdom of God', a vivid phrase that sticks in the mind. It is the one thing most people do remember from this passage. As a result, part of the baggage they have picked up is the notion that it is a sin for a Christian to be rich.

ANG: Well, as I say:

> There is a misconception regarding Christian morality which has become so widespread that it is regarded as a commonplace and seldom challenged. It is widely assumed that the attitudes to private property expressed in the

New Testament lend support to the doctrines of modern socialism. According to this view, Christ was a pacifist socialist and the early Christians were Communists. It is consequently inferred that every Christian should be a pacifist and a Communist, and that a Christian who is neither is failing to live up to the principles he professes.[23]

That was rather the line Fr Incledon took: he thought I was demoting the Christian vocation, which *is* to sanctity. Sanctity *all of us, all of us, all of us* are called to. When a lot of poor people leave the priesthood, or leave a religious order to take a lady, I say: 'Don't think you're opting for a soft option, because sanctity — as opposed to perfection — is what you're *always* called to. You set out to pursue it in one *particular* way by entering a religious house, but now that you feel psychologically compelled to leave, don't make that lower the vocation to sanctity, to which you are inevitably called.'

AH: I suppose what Fr Incledon and others are saying is that it's impossible to attain sanctity in any other state than poverty.

ANG: But it's perfectly untrue! I say again: people can lead highly unconventional lives, from St Lewis [sic] of France, who was king, and St Thomas More, the second most powerful man in the kingdom after Henry VIII, to Benedict Joseph Labre, all of whom achieved sanctity in *widely* different lives.[24] We don't read enough of those saints. Oh, and naturally, the Apostles, I've noticed, hadn't got a religious order to push their causes! I don't like — well, I mustn't say I don't like — I don't care for the way religious orders *press* for their members to be canonised, as they do!

AH: It's always been rather like supporting football teams, hasn't it?

ANG: Yes, that's right. I feel it about Newman, too. There is a whole *push*: 'Must get this done!' It leaves me cold, absolutely cold... Another two saints with very different vocations: St Philip Neri, who was regarded as Apostle of Rome — a *frightfully* corrupt Church and society and so on — and he *lives* in it, calling everyone to sanctity. St Benedict, on the other hand, having an *equally* corrupt and wicked Rome, pulls out, to become a hermit and contemplative... activated and inspired by renunciation of the world.[25] There again you get *quite different* vocations, both called to sanctity, both canonised by the Church. One of them deliberately pulling out of the world to try and make a sort of ideal society, emphasising he's not asking anybody to feel compelled to join him for the sake of their salvation. He pulls away from the fathers of the desert, who are holding up for *most* people an unrealisable ideal—living in the desert and eating dates! Making baskets!—but doing nothing apostolic *at all* in the way of going out to convert people (other than the Lord *intended us* to do, by praying for people). Yes, those three are very good examples of sanctity achieved by *quite* different means. St Philip Neri settling down in Rome up a pair of stairs and people coming to see him all day long—not a moment's peace!—and losing himself in the life of Rome, correcting all to a life of holiness.[26]

> Many people, when the distinction made by Our Blessed Lord is brought home to them, feel that a compromise is being made in which the demanding nature of Christian morality is being accommodated to the weaker brethren. This is largely because, in the universal atmosphere of egalitarianism in which we live, man has lost the concept of the absolute uniqueness of his own creation and vocation. He is tempted to measure himself against his fellow man and not against the uncreated Perfection of Almighty God, Who alone gives meaning to his life. He fails to appreciate that man achieves sanctity not necessarily by aspiring to a way of life which is objectively higher in itself, but by fulfilling the unique role which God has given him.[27]

AH: That passage, in which you mourn the loss of the 'absolute uniqueness' of the creation and vocation of each one of us, struck me more forcefully than anything else in *We Believe* when I first read the book. To me it was an inspiration. But inevitably, that concept must be watered down by those who hold that sanctity can only be achieved thus or thus.

ANG: Yes. I'm being *very* personal, making a confession to you, but I should never be a priest now if I'd been pushed through the *then* [c. 1924] extremely oppressive training of the clergy at the English College, instead of the Beda.[28] I'm sure I wouldn't have stayed the course. My inspiration is R.H. Benson.[29]

So there was I, having been brought up by the Jesuits... and feeling — this sounds like a criticism but it isn't — that there was something very inhuman about their complete extinction of personal place, which had meant a great deal to me...

Isn't it very amusing to see how the Jesuits and Benedictines, both great schools of saints... are *entirely* different in accidentals? The Benedictine vocation's whole life is tied to a place, and to being a member of a family. In theory at least, they never leave their abbey. They are supposed to have the family as very strong, the Father Abbot as a father... It comes out very strongly in that wonderful book published when Bishop Butler was Abbot of Downside, called *Benedictine Monachism*...[30]

Now at the other end of the scale the Jesuits emphasise mobility and flexibility. I won't say anything against the system for Jesuit priests, because I have a great admiration, the greatest admiration, for them, indeed. But it's absolute... We were brought up, you see, to think that any Jesuit might be sent to China tomorrow, and they were pushed about in the most extraordinary way. You came back to school and found whoever it was, a new priest, had started a new subject. It was all *terribly* impersonal and they put great emphasis on it. And it was one of the reasons, I think, why they, in the old days, being, of course, the biggest religious order — certainly in England — had so few breakdowns. Because: 'Oh, you're not happy as a Prefect at Beaumont. Let's see how you'd like to go to Glasgow.' There's all the difference in the world between their two emphases. The actual not accepting that call to the higher way of life is not *sinful*...

AH: So, to be clear, are you saying that if Francis of Assisi had felt his call to poverty but then said to God: 'No thank you, I'd really rather not. I'll just be a good cloth merchant like my father', that there would have been no guilt in that?

ANG: There's *no guilt* in choosing a lower than a higher way of life, unless it be sinful. We're all, of course, encouraged very *strongly* to deny ourselves, as we *must* do. Otherwise we shall be falling down to Hell. But an individual instance of self-denial can be absolutely free: I have managed to restrict myself to one course only every night at dinner, a constant reminder that we have to do many things that

Controversies 33

are certainly not binding under sin. But, as a matter of fact, I *have* made that commitment. Yet if some time this evening I get a really good blow-out, I won't have been *in sin* at all! . . .

AH: I'm sure that many people would be happy to accept the gist of what you have just said. But what about those people who believe that making money is a sign of virtue, and of God's blessing: the 'Prosperity Gospel', with the accompanying belief that if you're poor it's your own fault, due to your idleness and fecklessness?

ANG: [*Vehemently*]: That's a *blasphemy,* and an avaricious one! . . .

The eye of the needle comparison, for all its vividness, doesn't change the dialogue, on which I put so much emphasis, that he was doing *no wrong*. He asks: 'What must I do to be saved?' and is told: 'Keep the Commandments.' And he's very disappointed. He expected something much more challenging. But Our Blessed Lord of course *says*—well, it's a serious question!—*that is enough: you will save your soul.*

AH: Of course, if Our Lord were saying that rich people, simply by dint of their wealth, are automatically damned, that would not only conflict with the Church's constant teaching through the last 2,000 years, but would necessitate a line being drawn for the permissible maximum net worth, above which anyone whose assets exceeded it would forfeit their salvation.

ANG: We must always go back, you see, to the fact that *all through,* the immorality of what is under consideration is *your individual choice of will, not* the effects that the world sees. Our Blessed Lord says that a man who *lusts* after a woman has already committed adultery with her in his heart (Matthew 5:27–28) . . .

AH: Very hard teaching!

ANG: *Yes!* But . . . that *is* the teaching: that sin is in the will. It is not in actually *sleeping* with the woman. You see, people have this idea: an overt *act* is the sin . . . but think of St John with: 'He who hates his brother is a murderer' (I John 3:15).

AH: *Mens rea* rather than *actus reus.*

ANG: Yes. That's what we're talking about. We're not talking about the actual sexual act, which we all believe, of course, is a *very noble thing*. The heterosexual act is cooperation with Almighty God in the work of creation, one of the greatest gifts of God to man. And by the same token, celibacy is the necessary prerequisite for the other things we've been talking about: giving up all material things and renouncing your own will. You *can't* do that once you're begetting children.

I say all that in *We Believe*, how if you are a young bachelor with no one dependent upon you, going home late at night and finding a man leaping out at you from a dark doorway with homicidal intent, you can in that split-second say: 'I don't want to send this poor man to extremity, so I will turn the other cheek to the striker.' But if you were a *married* man, came home and found your wife being beaten up and the children killed, you couldn't. You've got a duty to go to their defence. So all these people who try and embarrass us by suggesting we're not living the Christian life entirely miss this point.

AH: In the Sermon on the Mount, Christ proclaims the Beatitudes. One of them is: 'Blessed are the poor in spirit.' (Matthew 5:3). There are many people among the poorest in this country, and in the rest of the world, who habitually spend some of the little they have on lottery tickets, in the mostly forlorn hope of becoming multimillionaires. Although financially poor, they plainly cannot be called poor 'in spirit'. In addition, some of them will be enviously indignant, as the tabloid press has recently encouraged them to be, at the fact that the man who runs the lottery earns up to two million pounds a year by actually working! Yet there are also some people who are multi-millionaires and billionaires who give generously to charity, live holy lives of prayer, and so on.

4. Are these good rich people poor 'in spirit', even though, like the rich young man, they have 'great possessions', which, via philanthropy, can often do more lasting good than any state bureaucracy?

ANG: That's *everything* that I've said in my little book. And the sin is *avarice: really thinking* that an accumulation of wealth is the whole purpose of human life. The sin is *there*. No, what *is* your business is: what is the state of your mind and heart?

AH: So would you agree with that Anglican bishop who recently criticised the lottery for encouraging—

ANG: Avarice! Encouraging avarice! Yes. It's putting the whole emphasis on the accumulation of material wealth. I think it's appalling. I don't know what he said, but I think the lottery is an *appalling* thing. It's that obsessive thought from which this generation suffers so extremely: 'something for nothing.' It's a very very debilitating disease of the human spirit...

And the same with all pornography is that, isn't it? It's encouraging the lewd side of our natures.

AH: I find it somewhat depressing that one can't walk through central London nowadays without frequently having to put one's eyes down to the pavement to avoid seeing something that is—

ANG: Suggestive. Yes, well one of the greatest helps to the life of chastity is the custody of the eyes. That's an *enormous* help. But what your eyes see goes straight into your brain, and the memory returns to it.

AH: The other thing I find particularly objectionable, as the father of a young boy who can read quite well now, are those cards in telephone boxes advertising prostitutes. Many of them nowadays have 'soft porn' pictures of the women, so that one can't make a phone call in central London in the company of one's children without exposing them to such filth.[31]

ANG: Surrounded by it!

AH: One can't keep these things away from them.

ANG: No, no. In the old days the father of a... Victorian home *could do a great deal*... as to what books came into the house, who read them, etc.[32]

We must all, we believe, *try* and lead *holy* lives, but the consequences of our doing so are not for us to know, and it's not for us to judge other people. It's hard enough to judge our own motives; other people's we can't begin to. It's not our concern.

Well, St Francis of Assisi himself, to take the classic example of a rich young man who gave up all his wealth to follow Our Lord's call to perfection, never wanted to found an order. He was just leading this life of extraordinary asceticism, and his followers followed his example. He was hooked on this idea that you had to give up everything, but when he went to get approval from the Pope, in the thirteenth century, he said: 'Oh, *no* no no!' He said: 'You've got to study theology if you want to be a priest.' And St Francis never *was*. But if you want to be a *priest*, well, you've got to study theology. If you're going to study theology, you've got to have books, and if you're to have books, you have to have somewhere to house them: you have to have a library. And the Pope insisted on that. And people said: 'Oh, he has saved us from that great *bane* of the Eastern Churches: a lot of meddling monks!'

AH: Even Jesus must have studied. He knew his scriptures well enough to dispute with the doctors in the temple at the age of twelve.

ANG: Yes, indeed! A very advanced child, precocious! Of all the silly stories, one that always sticks in my mind has Our Blessed Lady bearing the Divine Child in arms, appearing to a Franciscan, a Dominican and a Jesuit. And—oh! The Franciscan goes into *torrents* of expressed love, embracing the Child and embracing the Mother, oh yes, a *rhapsody*. The Dominican writes a very learned treatise on the Incarnation, distinguishing between the two natures and so on. And the Jesuit [*Putting on the high-pitched tone of voice of an excited connoisseur*]: 'That's a very promising boy you've got there!' [*Bursts into high-pitched laughter*]: 'Hope you get him in for Stonyhurst soon!'[33] [*More laughter, in which I share*] I do that well, don't I?

This is *really* the nub of what we're talking about. That a life of complete self-abnegation as practised by Our Blessed Lord, practised by St Francis in imitation of Him, is not, and cannot be, in the nature of things, coincident with Christianity. *Can't be*. If Christianity is meant by Almighty God to be the universal religion of mankind, it can't be interpreted in that way. It *can't be* ... As I say in my book, it would have died out in the first generation. The Catharists in the South of France—it seems St Dominic founded the Dominicans *very* largely to counteract their heresy—taught that everything, all matter in the physical creation *was bad*, and the whole Catholic tradition is: *'No no no!'* All that Almighty God has made is good, though our misuse of His gifts may lead us to sin. The proper use of them leads us to sanctity. All things by themselves, they're good *per se*.

I suggest very much in *We Believe* that the difference between Puritanism and Catholic asceticism is that the Puritan excludes many many aspects of life as being essentially evil, from wine to horse-racing to whatever you like, the theatre? 'Yes, oh they're evil!' A Catholic would always say: *'No no no!'* They're good, and *when we eschew them*, as strict religious do, we're giving up a good thing for a *better* thing. That's the essential difference between Puritanism and Christian *asceticism*.

> There is a difference between the modern sense of the word 'poverty', and the virtue we may term 'evangelical poverty', which is constantly counselled in the Gospels by Our Blessed Lord Himself. Poverty as popularly understood is destitution, ignorance, dirt and disease—the life of Shanty Town. There is nothing Christian in that and we are urged not to cultivate it, but to do what we can to eradicate it.[34]
>
> Evangelical poverty, as understood in the light of nineteen centuries of Christian practice, means that whatever our material circumstances, whether easy or hard, we should not attach undue importance to material well-being. Be prepared to be deprived of it if Almighty God so wills, and in no circumstances commit sin to achieve or preserve it.[35] Poverty in the sense of destitution cannot be a virtue. Poverty in the sense of detachment always is—and plainly the greater the detachment the greater the virtue. We can give things up willingly and thereby gain great merit.
>
> Consider St Francis of Assisi, who is always held up as the example of evangelical poverty and is always referred to as the poor man of Assisi. Yet he was a product of a very highly civilised and sophisticated society of which he had received all the cultural and educational benefits. Having benefited from the society of his time, he was doing a great and heroic thing when he stripped himself of all the material consequences of it and cultivated that complete detachment that expressed itself in an extremely ascetic and austere form of life. He could not and did not try to divest himself of the many advantages and benefits he had received.[36]

5. You say in *We Believe* 'The primary province for each of us is not the Third World but our own hearts.' You adapt Our Lord's rhetorical question: 'What doth it profit a man if he gain the whole world and suffer the loss of his own soul?' (Mark 8:36; Matthew 16:26) to 'What doth it profit a man if (though this obviously cannot be done) he gain the whole world *for Christ* and suffer the loss of his own soul?' And you say that 'the answer is again "Nothing", for each of us is brought into this world to establish the kingdom of God in his own soul. If we do that, we shall fulfil the whole purpose of our being.' You say you want to emphasise this 'because so much of our modern Christianity gives the impression that what we are here for is to put the world right.' You warn that 'To make a true contribution to putting the world right, we must first establish the kingdom of God in our own hearts.'[37] Yet when Our Lord speaks of Judgment Day, He has the damned asking: 'When saw we thee an-hungered, or athirst, or a stranger, or naked, or sick, or in prison, and did not minister unto thee?' And He says He shall answer them: "Verily I say unto you, Inasmuch as ye did it not to one of the least of these, ye did it not to me." And these shall go away into everlasting punishment'... (Matthew 25:44–46, KJV).

Does this not make plain that our salvation is actually *dependent upon* our willingness to serve Christ in the poorest of the poor, most of whom are to be found in the Third World?

ANG: Yes, certainly. [*A long pause*]. Why is it our duty? Because it's conducive to our salvation. It's our sanctification. Once again we're down to [*Quoting himself from earlier in our unrecorded conversation*]: 'results are not our business.' Results are not our business. What *is* our business is to decide to *give* our souls, minds and hearts *entirely* to Almighty God to direct as He will. And, amongst other things, to which He *does* direct us, are the Corporal Works of Mercy, to say nothing of the Spiritual Works of Mercy.[38] They're *essential*, in varying degrees according to one's vocation in life. And then it goes back again to something I emphasise so strongly in many places: that there's no meaning—and therefore no virtue—in the brotherhood of man unless it's rooted in the fatherhood of God. God enables us to be sons of the same Father.

But the emphasis, of course—I've put it here in rather challenging fashion—is *meant* to challenge that obsession of the present day that the Corporal Works of Mercy are what we're here for. They aren't. What we're here for is the sanctification of our own souls. What's this about? It's about our innermost selves. But the whole emphasis of the present day, which takes Christianity as *morality* and not as *truth*, is to get the whole proportion wrong, and think it lies in those *certain* Works of Mercy, which Our Lord does commend very strongly. Don't doubt that. But they're not what it's about.

The most philanthropic of benefactors in the midst of this world, his work has no value *in itself* at all: that's the results. But such work can be sanctifying. If it's done for getting recognition from his fellow man and buying a peerage from whoever you like, it's of no value at *all*. As a consequence of actions which result in him being saved, a man may *save* innumerable people from dying in the streets of Calcutta, but his motivation is different.

AH: Your mention of the man saving people from dying in the streets of Calcutta gives me the cue for another point I'd like to raise with you while we're on this question. Mother Teresa[39] has done exactly that. Yet when she came to England, she was moved by the sight of the homeless on our streets, and the fact of our permissive abortion law, which is tantamount to permitting abortion on demand. She said that we in England were in a way worse off, in spite of our material wealth, than those who suffer material poverty in the Third World. We condemn so many people, by the individualism and materialism of our society, she said, to miserable loneliness, to being cut off from any loving family, as from any sense of the presence of a loving God.[40]

ANG: [*Moved to compassion, with emotion*]: Yes. Oh yes, and she came out fighting. Of course, you know, she's not popular with the people who believe in *results* at all. She's not concerned—not *primarily* concerned—with sanitation or whatever it be!

AH: Which is why she was very strongly criticised as being a sort of 'crypto-fascist' on Channel 4's recent programme 'Mother Teresa: Hell's Angel.'

ANG: Yes. Of course, that phrase means absolutely nothing.

AH: I'm not sure the actual phrase was used, but the programme held that she was friendly with certain leaders loosely defined as fascist, whose corrupt regimes — regimes, it was alleged, which contributed to keeping in poverty the sort of people she was looking after — she never criticised. The inference was that while self-righteously enjoying the reputation of a saint, and imagining herself to be so very charitable, she had wilfully failed to grasp the nettle of what was causing this poverty. It was further implied that her friendly contacts with these dictators gave them a spurious respectability, which they exploited for PR benefit. The programme's makers perhaps took the same line as Eva Peron,[41] at least as portrayed in the well-known musical *Evita*. In that, disgusted at the superficiality, as she sees it, of certain upper-class people in raising money for charity by having fun at balls, she bursts out: 'I shall abolish charity!', meaning: 'I shall make it unnecessary. The state will provide.'[42]

ANG: 'I shall *abolish!*' ... What we suffer from is the idea that *material* circumstances are the only things that matter. You see, she can't abolish poverty. What does poverty come from? Well, any *number* of things. But first of all: human nature is corrupt. We're *all* of us selfish, self-seeking, good-for-nothing. Is she going to cure those things? Of course she's not! Surely you can't do it! ... [This attitude] ignores the fact that the root of *all* evil is the wickedness and pride of *individual human people*. They can be cured, so the worldly think, by education, and social circumstances, and all the rest. They can be cured. They can't be. But *all* evil, as all good, is within our own souls.

6. Tax Avoidance and Tax Evasion

There is more than one catechism. First came the old 'Penny Catechism' [first published 1889, reissued by the bishops of England and Wales in 1971 and later editions], which is the basis of *We Believe*. Although never out of print, it had become somewhat neglected in recent years, being superseded by a more recent presentation, *The Teaching of the Catholic Church, A New Catechism of Christian Doctrine,* by Fr Herbert McCabe OP of Blackfriars, Oxford.[43] This was the text used by one of your many successors as Chaplain, your undergraduate convert, the

Rev. Dom Christopher Jenkins OSB, for instructing converts in the 1980s. It was the book with which he introduced me to the Church's dogmas. It bears the *Imprimatur* of Dom Christopher's predecessor as Chaplain, Archbishop Maurice Couve de Murville[44] (for those unfamiliar with the term, this is 'a declaration that a book or pamphlet is considered to be free from doctrinal or moral error'. *We Believe* itself bears that of the Bishop of Salford).

In his catechism Fr McCabe poses the question: 'How can we fail in the exercise of justice?', and lists in his answer as one of the ways 'by tax evasion and *inequitable forms of legal tax avoidance*' [my italics]. The clear inference from the point about 'inequitable forms of legal tax avoidance' is that people like Lord Vestey, to cite the most extreme example, whose family is renowned for having devised a legal mechanism whereby it pays virtually no tax at all on its vast fortune, is committing a sin of injustice.[45] I have heard you defend Lord Vestey more than once, when he has been criticised in the press.

If Archbishop Couve de Murville was right to grant his *Imprimatur* to Fr McCabe, can you really continue to defend the Lord Vesteys of this world?

ANG: It's getting gradually *worse*, isn't it? But the fact remains, if you're working *within* the law, you cannot be accused of injustice.[46]... There is a *very very* loaded passage... There's no way, if you *have* accumulated wealth, that you have to give all *that* to the poor which is the consequence of your industry and skill.

Tax evasion, of course, if you mean by tax evasion *telling a lie*, of course it's wrong to tell a lie. But there's all the difference between tax evasion and tax avoidance. Tax avoidance is a colourless thing: I avoid that tax, legally. Whereas evasion is a form of deception.

What does he mean by an 'inequitable' form? Does he mean you're twisting the law, or are you *deceiving*? What's 'inequitable'? I think that's *very very* curiously put. It should never have been allowed to pass.

AH: I assume Fr McCabe is implying that clever accountants can find loopholes in the law that enable people like Vestey to avoid giving away any significant amount of their wealth to help the needy through taxation, e.g. through the welfare state and the NHS.

ANG: But... if what you're doing is legal, you're doing [*in a high-pitched tone of gentle exasperation*]: nothing *wrong*![47] You're merely pointing out that the law does not make the claim that people think it's making. No — that's a *terrible* bit of work: not only loaded vocabulary, but very *inaccurate and undefined*.

AH: I should point out that Fr McCabe has been awarded the highest accolade his Dominican Order can give: Master of Sacred Theology!

ANG: Well, he doesn't come well out of *that* little extrapolation! Those terms are undefined. But they're *heavily* laden.

AH: If you're right, it seems odd that the Archbishop of Birmingham should have given his *Imprimatur* to this book.

ANG: Yes. I think Fr McCabe very much an *enfant terrible*. Oh, for *years back* he's been tendentious. Obviously, with a Master of Sacred Theology it's not a very good thing to say this, but he's a *very very* tendentious man. I've been quarrelling with him for years. Many people have told me that he is.

> Justice means giving to each man what is his due. That due varies. The due of every man is the respect we owe to him as being a unique creation of Almighty God. In material things the due of each man is what he has honestly and justly acquired, whether he has earned it by his mental or physical labour or whether it has been lawfully transmitted to him. We have no right to take this from him.
>
> The wickedness of injustice lies in taking away from another person what is justly his. That is generally admitted as being sinful. When we do that, we are guilty of theft or robbery.
>
> Another reason why it is necessary to dwell on sins of injustice is that at the present day there is an inclination to consider that all we possess comes from society. That view is without foundation, since society of itself produces nothing at all. There is no such thing, to use that phrase which is constantly bandied about, as the national wealth, which, the users of the phrase contend, the State has the duty to distribute equitably among its members. A nation of itself can never produce anything.

All that there is, is what the individual members of the nation have produced.

Society has the right to take whatever proportion of the achievements of its members is essential for the fulfilment of its essential functions. When occasionally the burden of taxation is lightened for one class or another, the newspapers are inclined to pronounce it as 'the Chancellor makes a present' to the class concerned. What he is in fact doing is merely saying, 'I propose to take less of what you have produced than I have hitherto been taking.' He is in no position to give a present to others, having no resources from which to do so, other than what he has previously taken — rightly or wrongly — in tax.

Injustice does not become justice if done by the nation or the State. Robbery is no less robbery if it is committed by the State than by an individual. A predatory State undermines honesty and destroys the incentives to achievement. Much of the view of life which we have been discussing stems from the envy of others to which we are prone as a consequence of the Fall.[48]

7. The combination of proliferating nuclear arsenals in many countries with the increased frequency of earthquakes and famines in recent years, to name but three factors, cause many Christians to think that they are living in the 'last days' prophesied by Jesus:

> For nation shall rise against nation and kingdom against kingdom; and there shall be earthquakes in divers places, and there shall be famines and troubles: these are the beginnings of sorrows (Mark 12:8 [KJV]).

In addition there is his prophecy that:

> ... in those days, after that tribulation, the sun shall be darkened, and the moon shall not give her light,
> And the stars of heaven shall fall, and the powers that are in heaven shall be shaken.
> And then shall they see the Son of Man coming in the clouds with great power and glory. (Mark 12:24–26 [KJV])

The sun and the moon being darkened could foreshadow the aftermath of a nuclear war, when great clouds of dust and grit are blown up into the sky before the onset of a nuclear winter. The stars of heaven falling could be a first-century way of describing the after-effects of nuclear explosion. Although people have believed that Christ's second coming was imminent in the past, they lacked our unprecedented capacity for swift annihilation through our own weaponry.

Do you think we are living in the last days?

ANG: I would just say that all conjectures are profitless. We don't *know*. It may or may not be so. The world may end this evening. *In five minutes!* [*With sudden inspired playfulness*]: In five — *one*! It *may*! Yes! We'll always have that consciousness of the frailty of human life and achievement. You are like a candle: one blow from Almighty God and there's ... *nothing left*. We can go to new methods of destruction. Almighty God will let us destroy.

I start in *We Believe* by making a parallel very early, between the creative and conservative power of Almighty God.

> Almighty God brings everything into being, and He can equally extinguish everything, so that you can regard the creative power of Almighty God as the first of a whole series of conservative acts, while the conservative activity of Almighty God is a whole series of creative acts.
>
> [Aquinas's approach] helps us to understand that all things must not only be called into existence by Almighty God but must be kept in being by Him from moment to moment. Things do not become necessary in the philosophical sense by being called into existence — they remain as 'unnecessary', or 'contingent', as before their creation. If Almighty God did not keep things in being from moment to moment, they would drop back into the nothingness from which He drew them.[49]

8. The daily media diet of such things as violent assault, child abuse and murder, to name but three of the serious categories of crime, convinces me that we are, relative to forty, thirty, or even twenty years ago, living in a new Dark Age [*This part of the interview took place in 1995, so the most recent period I was*

referring to was the mid-1970s]. Yet when I say this to people under 40, their response is often: 'Oh, but I'm sure these things happened just as much in the past; it was just hushed up.'

What do you say to that assumption?

ANG: I think I can say, as a very old man, that it's *bunk*! The idea that these things were happening as frequently as they are now and just being swept under the carpet is *wholly* unfounded. The whole *mentality* of the period wouldn't allow it to happen.[50] I've said to you many times how, until the First World War, public opinion *supported* what was, whether it was acknowledged or not, a Christian ethic.

It came across of course very markedly over the way in which divorce came in, *very* gradually at first, always with some sort of peripheral reference to the guilty party and so on, and went on, and has gone on increasingly every day, until today, when you can almost get a divorce over the counter! There's no question of moral guilt, or innocence, under consideration *at all*.

And public opinion was universally — or *overwhelmingly* — in support of what we might call Christian morality, and poor Mrs Thatcher so wrongly labelled 'Victorian values' when she was defending them. They weren't Victorian values at all. They were *Christian* values, of which a Christian society, in which I was brought up, was *overwhelmingly* in favour. And so long as that was the case, one had to, I think, have the support of the social sanctions. You can't *now* support the social sanctions! Ladies of my mother's generation would not receive people who'd been divorced, and still less remarried. Didn't happen. And society as a whole took that line. And people who *had let go of* Christian morality, rightly, went out of society.

Once society ceases to support Christian morality, the individual *cannot*, and should not, apply a social sanction. It's wholly ineffective. It isn't morality that's changed. But so long as society supported, by and large, Christian morality, people really had a duty to support that society and coincide with it.

But now that's gone *completely*, so that poor dear mothers who are expected to allow their daughters to sleep with their boyfriends under their roofs can really do nothing, or very little. They can say: 'You can't do that here, dear!' Well, they'll go and do it somewhere else!

AH: Refusing to receive a divorcee seems rather uncharitable.

ANG: *You just did not do it.* A lady *did not invite* such people. You realise that there was much more of a stigma applied to it *by society*, not so much by Christian morality.

The reporting of divorce cases, one should remember, was a very very obscene business really. Someone had to be the guilty party and so on. I was always told — I don't know if there's any evidence for it — that it was Queen Mary who put down, or tried to put down the *appalling* reporting that there used to be in those days, of divorce cases.[51] And she *certainly*, of course, continued the social sanctions — not admitting them to the Royal Enclosure at Ascot. That was a social sanction all right![52]

AH: I can see the justification, perhaps, for excluding the guilty party, but what about the injured party? What about the innocent spouse, in most cases the wife?

ANG: She had no business to marry again, so to say. She was committing adultery by marrying again, if she did. And not a few didn't![53]

AH: Of course, there was no such thing in English law as an annulment [a declaration by the Church that what was thought to have been a valid marriage was not in fact so], whereas in a Catholic country, though the social sanctions would have been in place, for someone whose marriage had been *annulled*, it would have been a different matter. One would still have been admitted to the equivalent of the Royal Enclosure at Ascot, I presume?

ANG: Oh quite. And that, of course, caused great scandal at the time of the *Marlborough* case. It occurred during my days in Rome, in the 20s, when the *then* Duchess of Marlborough, according to her plea, had been forced to marry the Duke. Her hysterical American mother was going to throw herself off a lighthouse, or whatever it was, at the time — a skyscraper — if she didn't go through with the marriage. She had achieved her great social ambition of her daughter being proposed to by a duke, and she had been threatening that she was going to take her life in the most appalling circumstances if she didn't accept. And they went on living—I won't say happily—very *unhappily* for twenty years, until *she* had an affair with a French colonel who was in England... and of course French society *would not accept them*.[54] They were ostracised from that society in those days. And they wanted to continue to move about in those circles. And it was *she* who raised the issue of annulment on the plea of having been forced into it by her mother. And then, alas, the English press at once said: 'Of course you can always get a nullity if you're a duke and have society behind you.' But it wasn't *his* initiative at all. It was *hers*.

Now she *got* her nullity, and I presume they both achieved their social ambitions. I don't know. But *that's* what happened, and within three years she wrote a novelette, entirely exposing life under the attitude of the English press at the time.[55]

And of course, all this sets aside completely the idea that marriage vows *are sacred*. I remember so well, when I was a *very* young priest in my early days with the Bishop of Brentwood, whom I was very fond of indeed, and one of my greatest friends wasn't happily married. It was just a sort of post-war thing with him. And they had a child, and *she* was thinking of applying for a divorce to get the child. And my old bishop, who, of course, knew them—they were living in Essex—said: 'NO! Divorce is a *terrible* thing! The *idea* of trying to undo a bond that has God's sanction behind it!'

He wasn't a bit moved by the idea that we'd always believed—because I think it occurred in my mother's Spanish family—that divorce was *all right*, breaking the bond was all right, for a good reason, like the custody of a child. 'No!', said the bishop, 'No! It's *divorce* that's the bad thing! It's not cohabitation with someone. It's not adultery that we're raising the fuss about. It's this very solemn bond.'

And, of course, it applies to *vows*. You can't just say to your abbot: 'I can't fulfil the vows I've undertaken. It's too difficult, and I want to be freed from them.' I'm making an extension. He didn't, but I remember *so* well, his indignation was not about the prospective possibility of adultery or anything else. It was the *breaking* of a solemn bond sanctioned by Almighty God Himself! Just to say: 'No, we're breaking that bond!' I was very struck. You never hear this now, of course.

AH: Except from the Pope [then St John Paul II].

ANG: Yes, but you very seldom hear it from ordinary English public opinion. 'This has made a *very* difficult situation, causing a *great* deal of suffering to many people. How can we solve it in a manner to reduce the suffering as much as possible?' It's all about 'happiness'!

AH: As Newman said: 'It is not at all easy... to wind up an Englishman to a dogmatic level.'[56]

ANG: Very good phrase! It's very important. It's terribly good. The national character, what we're after all the time is: anything for a quiet life — a quiet and dangerous life... After all, we're reasonable people, and what we're trying to bring about is the solution of a difficulty with the *minimum* of pain to all the people concerned. That's really the very leadership now. Our life's losses aren't any more a problem.

9. In *We Believe* you ask us to:

> Think how many people there are in the world today who are absolutely miserable, questioning their own identity — a disease peculiar to our generation.[57]

Another disease peculiar to our generation is AIDS. It obviously also makes many people absolutely miserable.

Given the danger of infection through various forms of sexual contact, especially now that the combined forces of the universally available contraceptive pill and our permissive youth culture, as well as the growing acceptability of gay sex, encourage early and promiscuous sexual behaviour, do we not put at risk our children's lives if we fail to warn them of the dangers?

ANG: At what point should Christian parents teach their own children? I've been saying for years — 'tisn't practical with what the world says today — but: let them learn about it from the world of nature. All right, if you are fortunate enough to be brought up in the country, you can start by collecting eggs with your mother. That's the way to *all* children, I'm quite sure of that. If you're living on a farm, you *absorb* it, without there being a *moment* in which someone says: 'Now we're going to teach you about sex education.' You tell them about the facts of life. We're *surrounded* by images of sex: it's the way the world goes on!

But there's a whole presentation in Catholic piety, starting with the Hail Mary: 'Blessed is the fruit of thy womb, Jesus.' It seems there are many ways of *gradually* initiating a child. If you can't go round collecting eggs, at least *teach* the child a Hail Mary, and the child will want to know what that means, and why, when Our Blessed Lady conceived Our Blessed Lord, she was told to go into the hill country to tell Elizabeth, and there we go. It's a lovely, beautiful story of the Visitation. The child leaping in Elizabeth's womb, John the Baptist, who was conscious that the other lady was carrying God Himself.

I remember faintly, at home we got *absolutely nothing* of what I'm talking about *at all*. Nothing from my dear parents, nothing from *anyone*. And, you know, when I went to Beaumont, for the first time, another boy, a *very* nice boy, older than I, told me the so-called 'facts of life' while we were walking around the playground, not with a religious input, but what he *knew*.

I think, frankly, that it never occurred to me till a little late. No, I would like to have started a little sooner perhaps. But there we were living in the country, with lambing every year going on, and collecting eggs and all the rest of it! I think a little more should have been said about it. Well, what they say now, it's all so brutal, whereas in the Divine Infancy. . .

AH: That is all very well, but it leaves unanswered the dilemma posed by AIDS. As I see it, if we don't tell our children of the risks from certain sexual behaviours, they may die from it, perhaps killing others on the way. If we do tell them, at the age of 14, as is now [the late 1990s] being done in state schools, we put into their minds the idea of playing with a kind of fire that might not have otherwise occurred to them.[58]

Should we tell them or not?

ANG: It's all the way it's done. The *statement* of truth never does any harm at all. I'm always coming back, again and again, to: *can we have morality without Almighty God?* All discussion is carried on, *studiously* leaving God *out of it*! We never start with the Ten Commandments. And in public discussion, we're trying to reach *our* solution without the ground for it, all the time. And it always depends how it's taught.

One has to start with the concept of a Creator imposing a moral order. Yes, start with the Ten Commandments, it's as simple as that. Teach the Ten Commandments, and say: 'There is a moral order, a Creator, Who is the Very Good Himself. And *these* are rules *laid down* by the Creator, of which one is: sex may only be used for the proper purpose *for which He gives it*: procreation within wedlock.'[59]

Everything falls into place if you start *at the top*. Everything falls into place. It's no good thinking you can start at the *level* of practice, and then finding some sanction, or theory, or philosophy behind it. You're wasting your time! But the approach nowadays is: 'Now, here is a very complicated problem. How can we solve it? Can we solve it with the least infliction of human suffering?' The answer to that is: we don't *start* at that end. We start at the end of there *being* a moral order, stemming *immediately* from Him Who has brought us into being.

The whole of our moral order is that, *whatever gift we're given*, it is to be used for the purpose for which He gave it. Whether it's physical health, or mental equipment, or good looks, whatever they are. He gives them, he *showers* a lot of gifts on the human race, always with a *quite unique* balance, and these gifts are *good* things, to be used for the ends for which He gives them.

The whole of the argument of this question is summed up by a single answer in the Catechism — *a wonderful work!* — the first question which the book asks: 'Who made you?'

'God made me.'

[*Playfully childlike*]: 'Why did God make you?'

'He made me to know Him, and love Him, and serve Him in this world, and to be happy with Him forever in the next.' It's *wonderful*! Because, of course, from the beginning, it *emphasises* that what we're *made for* is happiness — oh, but not here! You can't *expect* it before you leave here, because *only* God can fulfil all the desires of your mind and will. He *alone* can. But you won't *achieve* that until you pass from this world to the next. Meanwhile, before passing from this world, know Him, and love Him. And then to desire what He desires, so fulfilling *only* those desires that are good. And thereby, we shall be serving Him. Yes. It's all there. It's no good saying: 'Well, we'll put all that aside'! *No.*

So many so-called Christians now don't *believe* in revelation. They think Christianity's about a nice way of life, leaving out completely the plan of the Creator.

AH: 'Accept the ethics, can't stand the mumbo-jumbo', as Clement Attlee put it.

ANG: Well, yes. In essence, it's trying to achieve a morality without God. As simple as that. In contemporary society we're all liberal humanists now, and whoever you're speaking to you can take for granted that *he* is a liberal humanist, and you must take it for granted that he will expect you to be one...

I've said to you in many, many ways, there's no *hope* of getting agreement from our neighbour when we start with completely different springboards. If you don't start with a Creator, Who has made Himself known to us, what do you want? I think we make a great mistake in trying to establish what we believe in the sphere of morality without the reasons for believing it, which derive from God's revelation.

AH: I also think that if one tries too much to speak the language of the enemy, one starts to—

ANG: —think the thoughts of the enemy. Yes. It's a waste of time, and we're doing *so* much of that now. It's at the back of a lot of our own propaganda. Trying to make people see the [*in a heavily ironical tone*]: *reasonableness* of what we believe. To *them* it's just the latest mumbo-jumbo...

It all came out so markedly in that great conference at Cairo.[60] All the best people in the world were brought together to solve the problems of other members of the human race. And then when they had come from all over, the post of General Secretary [of the UN, then Dr Boutros-Boutros Ghali (sic)] was no good to us.

I think we should begin there: we're starting from *completely* different points of view from those of our neighbours. And that's the only thing to try and establish: that we start by believing in an all-powerful and all-wise Creator, Who has *revealed* his plan.

10. Your undergraduate convert Dom Christopher Jenkins, when Chaplain at Cambridge, stated that the Church's teaching that it is a sin to use artificial contraception was not a 'membership issue', i.e. that conscientious objection was possible for good Catholics. This teaching on birth control is not *ex cathedra*, unlike, for instance, the dogma of the Assumption of the Blessed Virgin Mary into heaven, which to reject is to cut oneself off from the Church. [*Contrary to this argument, there are circumstances in which contraceptive pills can act in an abortifacient manner. This happens when they fail, as sometimes happens, to prevent conception. The abortifacient effect then occurs by blocking the implantation of an embryo in the lining of the womb. Given this fact, no Catholic should ever use them, with the exception of women who are not in a sexual relationship, who may use them to help with premenstrual syndrome, acne and some other health conditions.*]

This teaching on contraception is one of the greatest barriers to people taking the Church seriously, and therefore to the conversion of many people who might otherwise consider becoming Catholics. In my own case, it was initially an obstacle that I had to overcome before requesting instruction in the Faith from Dom Christopher as an undergraduate convert, and I accepted Dom Christopher's 'conscientious objection' position [I have since accepted the Church's teaching]. Yet Pope John Paul II has refused to relax the Church's position as stated in *Humanae Vitae* (1968) any jot or tittle. In fact, he has frequently re-emphasised it, having himself been one of those responsible for drafting Pope Paul's encyclical.

Contrary to popular belief, the document, which caused great outrage when it was published, both in the press and in liberal Catholic circles, was not by any means a new development, but a restatement of the Church's consistent tradition, a tradition which, until 1930, was shared by the Church of England. But if Dom Christopher is right—and his approach is shared by the vast majority of Catholic clergy in this country, including the hierarchy [*this was true at the time of the interview in the late 1990s; it is somewhat less widespread now, especially among younger priests*]—shouldn't the fact that conscientious objection on this point is an option be more widely publicised, in the interest of making more conversions?

ANG: [*Very long pause*]: Sex is a gift. It's a gift that we believe has been given *primarily* for one purpose, because we live through that one purpose. There's a simple answer. *No one* considers that, of course, and all this absurd discussion goes on against the background that everyone has a right to get all the sexual pleasure out of life that they can.

AH: It's absolutely mad to suggest otherwise, they think.

ANG: Well, we've been taught that for 100 years, both by the press and other agencies. 'It's the only pleasure people have: let them all have it!' But once you say you can be *entirely responsible* about your exercise of it!... You *can't* be responsible about *any* of the gifts that God has given you. 'I'm going to have as much as — *dollops upon dollops* of anchovy toast [which he and I were eating as we spoke], and I'm going to sleep twenty-four hours round the clock, and I'm not going to get up and do any work today' — you could go on forever! If every whim were carried out to extremes, plainly there'd be no *duty* in it at all, whereas we *do* believe there's *duty* about all this. There's *duty* about our exercise of our natural gifts.

God, in His wisdom, is still going to take you as though you were a *reasonable person*. No, you are a *reasonable person*, and *all* morality must consist ultimately in making your will coincide with the will of Almighty God. *He's* the only judge of whether you've conformed!

I'll give you another example — comes in *We Believe* — about Roman vomitoria:

> Here is another comparison which may help to make clear the wickedness of getting the pleasure of an act whilst excluding the possibility of the consequence for which that act is intended by Almighty God. The Romans, we are told — though it is hard for us to imagine the mentality that allowed them to act in that way — ate and drank until they could hold no more and then made themselves sick in order to have the pleasure of eating and drinking again.

That is the perfect parallel to what we do when we exercise our sexual gifts and yet exclude the possibility of their resulting in the purpose for which Almighty God intended them. Food and drink are given to us so that we may replenish our bodily strength. So long as we are not excluding the possibility of its nourishing us, it is right to take pleasure in eating and drinking. There is nothing wrong or sinful about it. When we start eating and drinking solely for pleasure, as in the Roman example I have given you, the attempt to obtain the pleasure while excluding the purpose for which it is given is sinful.

In exactly the same way masturbation, homosexuality and the practice of artificial birth control exclude the very possibility of conception taking place.[61]

11. It is incumbent on the Church to explain and clarify her teaching as much as possible, in order to help the faithful both understand and follow it with informed obedience. Pope John Paul II, while never diluting the teaching on contraception, has emphasised the importance of this duty to explain and clarify. But in spite of his and others' best efforts, many people still find it hard to accept the teaching. Their problem with it is this:

Why should natural methods be permitted, and artificial ones forbidden, when their *intention* is the same?

ANG: Ah, but of course, as soon as you say that, you're putting things in the wrong order. Your intention in using natural contraception *is* to prevent the consequence of your action. But it's not actually *doing* anything to thwart the course of nature. [*Long pause*]. Anyway, you can go on having sexual contact with your wife long after she's past child-bearing. There's no reason why you shouldn't have. You're not thwarting a natural purpose.

AH: But even if you say that with natural contraception you are cooperating with the natural faculties of your wife's body, you are still taking deliberate steps to prevent her from getting pregnant. Isn't that the same thing *in principle* as using artificial contraception?

ANG: No. This *all* comes back to the different springboard. The Church starts with an omniscient, all-powerful Creator, who has set us here for one purpose, and *made* it all absolutely clear. The reign of God is not a democracy! 'This is what I would have done. I would have done this in the first place, had I been Creator.' I dare say you wouldn't! But this sort of nonsense makes the entire discussion wholly impossible! So you *weren't* Creator!

AH: Even Paul VI was aware, as he put it, in a classic of papal understatement, in *Humanae Vitae*, that 'It is to be anticipated that not everyone perhaps will accept this particular teaching.'[62]

ANG: Never fear to be in a minority. *Never*.

12. We are told in the Bible that whilst 'man looks on the outward appearance, the LORD looketh on the heart.' (I Samuel 16:7). If the essential part of a human being is internal and invisible, then, given the trouble caused to Christians by sexual temptation, — including, sadly, not a few priests, even though they take Communion several times a day — in the words of the Jesuit poet Gerard Manley Hopkins: 'To what serves mortal beauty?'[63]

Or: why did God make some people so physically attractive, given the danger to our souls?

ANG: [*Matter-of-factly*] To encourage procreation. Without that natural enjoinment — the other to eat — no procreation would take place. Sounds so awful! 'Increase and multiply!'[64] That, to the liberal humanists, is *absolute anathema!* '"Increase and multiply!" Two thirds of the world's population is starving, and you tell us to increase and multiply?!' Oh yes, that'd have them foaming at the mouth! They think we're absolutely mad because we're always bringing in a religion which they don't share.

AH: That's true, and very few of them ever bother to ask: 'What is the *basis* for your beliefs?' They just assume Catholicism is superstitious rubbish, sometimes producing statistics to bolster their assumption. Yet the statistics are often dishonest, inaccurate or both.[65]

ANG: If we believe in an all-wise and all-powerful Creator we *cannot but* believe that He's provided the means of support for us. We cannot *but*. It's a question obviously of production and distribution, and God knows what else.

13. In *We Believe*, in your chapter on confession, you play down the role of feeling in religion:

> Sorrow for sin is an act of the will. I have already emphasised that on the last day we shall each be judged only by the use we have made of our own mind and our own will, the two things we can control. We can control our feelings only very slightly and at most indirectly. We are never bound to feel anything at all.[66]

Many of your readers, I am sure, will share the reaction of a friend of mine to this passage, who thought you had been too dismissive of the role of feeling in the life of prayer.

ANG: Both mind and will must be all the time subject to the mind of Almighty God... Well, do you mean they think [*floundering somewhat in puzzlement*] religion is about... having nice feelings?

AH: Or even *nasty* feelings, but some sort of feeling. Not that it is the essence of religion, but that it is essential to much of our experience and practice of it.

ANG: But we can't *control* our feelings, that's the point. It's a good thing if you *can* get your feelings to coincide with your will, *excellent*, by all means *do*. But, well, I drew this out talking to a correspondent, when I said... wasting my time at Cambridge as an undergraduate, I'm sorry, because I think that waste of time was *sinful*, and thus I must be sorry for my sins. I don't *regret* it! In the sense that it bore an *enormous* return, an enrichment of life, in many ways. And that, of course, applies equally to sins of the flesh, and so on. People think: 'I've got to wish I hadn't.' Yes, in one sense, because if you persist in that course you go to Hell. But to say: 'I didn't enjoy it' is nonsense. I *did*!

And I look back, saying: 'I *did*, and were it not for Hell, I would very likely return to the practices which I've now abandoned because I know they're wrong, and they're going to destroy me utterly in this world and the next.'

That's the answer to the question of people thinking we can enjoy *every* sexual activity without feeling guilty about it. We do *know* that in fact it does wreck people's lives, as gluttony does, as ambition does. They *do* ruin people. We *know* that, but it isn't to say that one doesn't, or hasn't, enjoyed them. My *propensity* towards evil…'Yes, I *have* done such and such, but I *know* it's wrong, and I know it's destructive. I know it's going to disrupt me altogether in this world and the next'.

AH: After all, if sin were no fun, who'd bother with it?

ANG: [*Mutual laughter*]: Yes! Never deny, I've enjoyed having, oh, three more than I should to drink and so on. I've enjoyed it every bit! Jolly enjoyable! But to say: 'I *don't* enjoy' — it's not *true*!

The truth — wait a minute [*He asks me to read aloud the epigraph from* We Believe].

AH: 'Truth alone is worthy of our entire devotion.'

ANG: And to be hypocritical about what we're talking of… is not *true*.

[*Intensely*]: And you *never feel* anything as being done for Almighty God. You're doing it because the Truth comes before everything, and you *know* that your duty is to *try* and bring your *mind* to His, and your will to His… It *isn't* just an agreeable emotion. A simple example, of course, was the death of George V [reigned 1910–36], of blessed memory: '**Duty**, duty, duty.' Runs through the whole [of his reign].

When I try to look back on life — it's a wonderful thing, isn't it? — it's an *objective* thing. It's not *feeling*!

14. Jesus Christ is unmistakably portrayed in the Bible as someone Who warmly welcomed the outcasts of society, in a way that marked him off from the tradition of wandering holy rabbis in which He walked. His harshest words, by contrast, were reserved for the socially elevated priestly caste of the Pharisees, the 'whited sepulchres' (Matthew 23:27, KJV). And St Paul writes:

Ye have put off the old man with his deeds;
And have put on the new man, which is renewed in knowledge after the image of him that created him: Where there is neither Greek nor Jew, circumcision nor uncircumcision, Barbarian, Scythian, bond, nor free: but Christ is all in all (Epistle to the Colossians 3:9–11, KJV).

In the light of Christ's example and these words from the Apostle, should a Christian belong to a club such as the Travellers, whose membership is limited to people drawn from the upper and upper-middle classes? Would not an eccentric Jewish carpenter-turned-rabbi of extreme religious views and apparently violent temper be blackballed?

ANG: At the root of that question is egalitarianism again. But it's a lie! It's a lie! It's a lie! It's a lie! It's a lie! Egalitarianism, it's a lie followed by an impossibility.

A) It is not true.
B) Egalitarianism goes on to say: 'Well, if they're not, they must be *made* so.'

But that is an impossibility. Can't be done.

So, egalitarianism, a hundred times: first of all a lie, backed by an impossibility.

Now I want to go back, or we'll get to nowhere. [*Long pause for thought*]: What do you think of St Paul, if you look at St Paul as a whole: 'And he gave some apostles, and some prophets, and other some evangelists, and other some pastors and doctors'?[67] Or go back to Our Lord's relationship with the Jews: He *started* with the chosen race. Or the Transfiguration: a **wonderful**, *wonderful*, *wonderful* picture of the Church and the faithful. Yesterday was the Feast of the Transfiguration, when Our Blessed Lord revealed Himself as God to only *three*, *three* disciples, chosen out of twelve.

AH: 25 percent!

ANG: Yes. No equality there at all.[68]

15. The greatest obstacle, apart from her teaching on contraception, for many people to their considering becoming Catholics, is the history of deliberate, systematic cruelty committed by the agents of the Church, sometimes justified and authorised by certain popes, in pursuit of her mission to save souls. Indeed, a woman who [at the time of the interview] may well be your only surviving exact contemporary 'student' from Cambridge, Frances Partridge, has said: 'I can see that religion works for individuals, but appalling things have been done in its name — the Inquisition, the religious wars, the terrible problems in Ireland, and so on.'[69]

How do you answer this objection?

ANG: [*He refers me to his talk 'Fundamentals and Accidentals'. He once gave it to a group of Catholic graduates at Oxford in 1968*]:

> It is necessary for us to appreciate how misleading may be the distinction between the Church and the World. The antithesis which we set up between them is a false one. There is in fact no such dichotomy. It is rather like the traditional distinction between the Soul and the Body. In both cases the terms are perfectly acceptable as long as we do not think of two disparate entities brought together. In this life man is one single indivisible being living on two planes at once, which are interdependent and constantly interacting on each other.
>
> So with the Church and the World. They are not two separate, self-contained entities, facing one another. They are inter-penetrating, inter-acting, since the same people belong to both. Every child of the Church is also the child of his own age, thinking its thoughts and influenced by the culture and environment which that age provides. The Church is constantly influencing the current scene not by exerting pressure on it from outside but because her members, who through their membership of her are citizens of the heavenly Jerusalem, are also at the same time actors on the contemporary stage.
>
> I recall in this connection a remark made to me when I was a student at Rome in the heyday of Fascism: 'Always remember that the next Pope but five is a member of the Ballila' (the Mussolini Youth into which all Italian boys were enrolled). Of course he was. How could he not be?[70] Just as at this moment the next Archbishop of Westminster

but five is now being indoctrinated in all the orthodoxies of the welfare state in a state school.

We cannot, if we would, jump out of our skins or escape the influence of our age. In more liberal times it was easier for some to contract out and try to form (as they thought) pockets of more rational or Christian living. Such experiments are liable to be condemned by a collectivist age as a sort of escapism. They have much in common with the call of the desert and the cloister, states of life providentially designed for those whose vocation goes that way. Each of these is a voluntary society, but the Church is not and can never be. She is designed by the same Providence to be the one Ark of Salvation for all.

Once we have seen her in that light no likes or dislikes can affect our compelling duty to belong to her. She can never be selective in her membership (as can a religious order). Nor can she be an ivory tower. Involvement (to use the current jargon) is not for her a virtue: it is inescapable. And so, in every age, we see her members entertaining, frequently adopting and even blessing, but always ultimately discarding the current orthodoxies. This is a process which must be seen as both inescapable and transient. It is the price we pay for the Incarnation. The mistake is ever to attach undue importance to the process and above all to imagine it final and enduring — to think that the Church has at last found the ideal material framework in which to express the unchanging truth. This is a temptation which assails equally, let us say, those who idealise the achievements of the thirteenth century and those who idealise the aggiornamento of today. The Church will work in and through a social or political or even ideological system as long as she can and then, when it appears to be strangling her or when she is in danger of being identified with it, she will shake herself free. Then the snapping of familiar ties may both bring much pain to her children and cause her to be regarded by others as the most unreliable of allies.

How many old-fashioned French Catholics, who had been brought up to believe in the union between the throne and the altar, must have felt cut adrift from their moorings when Leo XIII made his overtures to the Third Republic? The swing between involvement and disentanglement is a constant if irregularly working pendulum. Pius XI at the time when he was making concordats with the dictators, is reputed to have said that he would make a bargain with the Devil himself if he could thereby serve the interests of the Church. Less than a century earlier Pius IX had declared that the Church had no need to come to terms with the nineteenth century. Neither the example of dissociation from, nor that of alliance with, the contemporary world may arouse much enthusiasm in a liberal Catholic today. They may serve to show how pragmatic the Church can be and to demonstrate an underlying consistency beneath superficial disparities. The process is one repeated again and again throughout the centuries, for in one form or another the Investiture controversy is always with us. There is always a price to pay for worldly support and worldly status and often the moment will come when the price is found too high.[71]

16. Finally, Alfred, can you tell me what, in all your long life, has been your happiest moment?

ANG: I didn't always appreciate that happiness is a matter of the *will*. [*Scornfully*]: It's not a number of feelings. My dearest child, one doesn't distinguish between them. Each stage of one's life is just like every other one! It's so silly, but for a Christian to define happiness, if you mean the most *important* to him, the greatest are those when you *receive most*.

AH: What about the time when you felt the most—

ANG: [*Interrupting irritably*]: No! Not feelings! Feelings only *help me* towards happiness. You have to *make* happiness! But, looking back over my 94 years, what is the most *important* thing, from the point of view of what it *gave* me? Ordination to the priesthood—yes! That's *will*, not feeling! Happiness isn't anything to do with your feelings. Having *peace of mind*.

AH: But the day of your ordination was the occasion of your commitment to a lifelong and, many would think, onerous duty.

ANG: Well, yes. They're strangers to the truth. The most

important thing in the world is truth. 'Truth alone is worthy of our entire devotion.'[72] And being ordained a priest gives you the status to spread the truth. Well, that's what you're ordained for. So that's how I define happiness.

But they ask a silly question. I mean, what do they mean? 'Have a nice day!' [*In a deliberately high-pitched, precious voice*]: 'Have a *nice* day!' You know my answer, don't you? 'No', I say, 'I have *quite* other plans.' Is that a good answer? Happiness is what you make it!

Are you trying to do the will of Almighty God or aren't you?...

It's no good thinking you're going to find happiness indulging *any* pleasure at all. It doesn't lie that way.

AH: It's one of the most wonderful phrases of the American Declaration of Independence: 'life, liberty, and the pursuit of happiness.'[73]

ANG: Yes! Yes! That's an absolute pot of nonsense! Happiness, I should say, the contemplative spirit, is achieved by trying to discover and perform the will of the God who brought it into being![74]

AH: One could perhaps adapt it to '*eternal* life, *divine* liberty and the pursuit of happiness *with God*.'

ANG: Well, then they should *find* it! Hoping 'to be happy with Him forever in the next.'[75] Yes! That's what they've left out because there they are, throwing away any concern with the Creator... and trying to find happiness *inwardly* without discovering what the mind of the Creator wants and what He created us for: the Truth. Come back to the Truth *every* time and you can't be disappointed.

And producing in all these people, which the Gospel does produce, a decent mind, contentment. That's it. But if you do throw the Creator out at the beginning of the argument, where the hell can you *get* to?

NOTES

1. Letter from Alfred quoted in Gregory-Jones, *A History of the Cambridge University Catholic Chaplaincy 1895–1965*.

2. The Oxford and Cambridge Club finally admitted women as full

members in April 1996, shortly after our conversation on the topic. In 1993, members had voted against full membership for women, allowing only 'non-voting associate' membership and continuing to bar them from the library and bar. In 1995, the heads of all but four of the seventy-three Oxford and Cambridge colleges resigned in protest at the ban on women, who were then 40 percent of the students at both universities. A group of members then campaigned successfully to admit women. Source: Anonymous. 'Oxford & Cambridge Club Elects First Female Member', *The Chronicle of Higher Education*, April 12, 1996.

3. Surprising as it may seem, Alfred's statement is quite accurate. Before the University agreed, without a vote, on December 6, 1947, to admit women on the same terms as men, the women, though they studied at the University, though they attended the same lectures and some social events as the men, were not members of the University. Their degrees were granted by their colleges, which were independent institutions. The first woman to receive a degree was the Queen Mother, who was awarded an honorary degree in 1948. It seems somehow fitting that Alfred should have failed to recognise her when he met her on the stairs of the Travellers Club!

4. In 1920, Oxford University admitted women to full undergraduate status, with the right to have degrees awarded by the University. In the same year, Cambridge undergraduates, of whom Alfred was then one, voted by 2,329 to 884 to maintain the status quo, the Union by 365 to 266. 'Women cannot be admitted on equal terms because they are not content with equality', said the Master of Corpus Christi. 'They mean to rule and usually do in the end.'

On December 8, 1920, the University (the dons and Senior Members) voted to reject full membership for women by 904 votes to 712. Resident MAs voted in favour by 214 to 191, but non-residents swung the vote the other way. The historian Eileen Power left Girton for LSE. The vote 'left women's position in the University exactly where it was. I've never felt so bitter in my life.' *CAM* (Cambridge Alumni Magazine), Easter Term 1998.

5. By the term 'the visible creation', Alfred implies the Catholic belief in the invisible, that of angels and demons.

6. 'After both Girton and Newnham alumnae petitioned the University for membership, "titles of degrees" were proposed for women instead of "tripos certificates." Economist Alfred Marshall ten years earlier in 1887 had thwarted new attempts to secure women's degrees and insisted that leisured women should live with their parents. More of them in Cambridge would be "detrimental to discipline." Marshall now led the opposition. A woman's job, he said, is primarily household management, so "concentration of all her energies on merely intellectual work for three

or four years is far from being the unmixed gain to her that it is to young men." Women's "lower intellectual potential" means they are diligent at best, drawn to Cambridge less by education than by 2,000 eligible men.'

'Eleanor Sidgwick, wife of Trinity philosopher and agnostic Henry Sidgwick (1838–1900), who had helped initiate lectures for women already living in Cambridge, and who had complained after Marshall's previous successful attempt to stop women's membership that the University had "become hidebound in a sort of stupid conservatism," countered that 50 percent of middle-class girls didn't marry anyway [can this figure have been correct?]. They need to earn a living, she asserted, or involve themselves in the world beyond their families, not bury themselves in trivia and domestic chores. [Alfred would have criticised the assumption that a housewife's role is trivial as demeaning]. Every woman, said Mrs Sidgwick, needed a room of her own to work, she claimed, with "no clashing calls of duty."'

'Two months of acrimonious debate were reported blow-by-blow in the national press. Undergraduates again rejected the idea of opening the University to women, by 2,137 to 298, the Union by 1,083 to 138. On May 21, 1897 came the final vote. Walls were plastered with posters reading, in huge red letters, 'Down with Women's Degrees' and 'Beware the Thin End of the Wedge.' Undergraduates transported non-resident MAs from the station to vote at the Senate House at breakneck speed, and crowded onto rooftops, window ledges and lamp-posts. At first, MAs awaiting the result in Senate House Yard were only pelted with flour, eggs and confetti thrown from Caius College. But at 2pm, at a simulated cock-crow:'Cooped up like sheep in a pen, the devoted dons, some thousands in number [really?], were pelted with fireworks of every description, while the smoke rose in clouds above their heads. The noise of the explosions and the cheers and counter-cheers were deafening.' (Source: an anonymous observer, quoted in Rita McWilliams-Tullberg, *Women at Cambridge: A Men's University — Though of a Mixed Type* (London: Victor Gollancz, 1975, 138–139.) 'When finally announced, the vote refused women "the title of degrees" by 1,707 to 661; resident MAs voted against by 320 to 149. Frustrated in their victory rampage through Newnham by Nora Sidgwick's quick action in barring the gates, the undergraduate mob tore down doors, shutters and fences and started a huge bonfire in Market Square. Even a brewer's dray was pitched onto the flames.'

'By 1900, when Henry Sidgwick, the founder of Newnham Hall (as it then was) died, there were 165 students at Newnham and 180 at Girton. Women were still unable as of right to attend lectures, use libraries or borrow from the University Library. To put this in context, it was only in 1882, by the Married Women's Property Act that women were for the first time permitted incomes independent of their husbands.' Felicity Hunt and Carol Barker, *Women at Cambridge: A Brief History* (Cambridge University Press, 1998).

7. Alfred went up in October 1920. The riot he describes took place on October 20, 1921, the beginning of his second year. By the Representation of the People Act of 1918, brought in by Lloyd George's wartime Coalition government, female householders over thirty finally achieved the vote in parliamentary elections. Women could now become MPs but still not Cambridge undergraduates. Ballots at the University agreed by 1,012 to 370 to grant women the 'title of degrees', but wider participation in university life was once again denied them. Male undergraduates, still the only kind, raced to Newnham and, with a handcart, wrecked the bronze gates commemorating Miss Clough (Anne Clough, 1820–92, Principal of Newnham 1875–92, collaborator with Henry Sidgwick of the North of England Council for Promoting the Higher Education of Women). *The Daily Telegraph* confidently predicted: 'We shall not have long to wait before Cambridge falls into line with the rest of the world.'

In 1972 King's, Clare and Churchill were the first hitherto all-male colleges to admit women. Soon, contraceptive machines began to appear in JCRs and gate hours began to be ignored. How many babies, one wonders, have been aborted as a result? How much premature emotional disturbance has been wrought to young lives by adding the pressures of 'relationships' to those of academic and social competition? How much distraction from study and prayer? How much dissipation of productive intellectual energy? To ask these questions is not to dismiss the academic achievements of women, merely to query their cost.

Magdalene, in 1987, was the last college to admit women. The University had forever given up its power to limit the number of women students. A group of Magdalene men carried in solemn procession a mock-up coffin painted with the name of the college. *CAM* (Cambridge Alumni Magazine), Easter Term issue 1998.

8. Rev. Alfonso Manuel de Zulueta (Count de Torre Diaz), M. A. Oxon; b. 6th Feb 1903; s. of Alfonso Maria, 4th Count Torre Diaz (d. 1951) and Ana Marie, d. of Don Antonio Ruiz Tagle; educ. Ampleforth; New College, Oxford; Fribourg; Rome; at St James's Spanish Place, Marylebone 1931–39; Chaplain to Catholic undergraduates at Oxford 1939–41; Spanish Place 1941–45; Parish priest, Holy Redeemer, Chelsea 1945–80; 1st Chaplain to Challoner Club (a Catholic social club in London). D. 13th June 1980. Known affectionately to some of his congregation as 'Fr Zulu.' *Catholic Who's Who*, 1952, and the late Bishop Emeritus Patrick Casey.

9. Later the Rt. Rev. Mgr. Vernon Cecil Johnson, M. A. (Oxon); b. 1886; Educ: Charterhouse; Trinity College, Oxford 1905–08; Ely

Theological College; ordained in Church of England 1910; Curate of St Martin's, Brighton 1910–13, until he joined the Society of the Divine Passion, Plaistow; 'Father Vernon' was a well-known Anglican preacher; received into the RC Church 1929 by Fr Vincent McNabb O. P. (whose words form the epigraph to *We Believe*); studied at Beda College, Rome (like Alfred); Priest of Diocese of Westminster 1933; Chaplain to Catholic undergraduates at Oxford 1941–47; Domestic Prelate to His Holiness (Pius XII) 1951. Publ. as an Anglican devotional books, including *Happiness* (1926), many times reprinted; as a Catholic, *One Lord — One Faith* (1929), *The Message of St Theresa of Lisieux* (1936). *Catholic Who's Who* and Trinity College Archives, Oxford.

10. Many readers will be puzzled, surprised or even shocked by Alfred's dismissive reference to the 'so-called refugees from Franco.' To explain this remark and put it in perspective, please see Appendix I: *Alfred and Franco*.

11. 'The Board' is the Oxford and Cambridge Catholic Education Board, the authority, directly subject to the respective bishops, which controls the Chaplaincies at the ancient universities.

12. 'On April 30, 1965, the Fisher Society, the undergraduate body that had always, up to that point met with the Chaplain as its President, passed the following motion: "It is the wish of this Society that Roman Catholic women undergraduates and postgraduates of the University be eligible for full membership". The motion was carried by 37 votes to 4.'

The President of the CUCA [Cambridge University Catholic Association], Hamson, wrote in June to the Secretary of the Board:... 'suggesting that, "perhaps members of the sub-committee [constituted to elect a new Chaplain and to oversee a potentially difficult period of transition] might be able to recommend to the Board that at the next incumbency the Cambridge Chaplaincy became a joint Chaplaincy for men and women *in statu pupillari* as the Oxford Chaplaincy has long since been. The Board's subcommittee was indeed considering this possibility.'

'When Monsignor Gilbey tendered his resignation, he did so on a question of authority. His final letter to the Board was written on July 15, 1965 (after he had been lunching with Cardinal Heenan) [1905–1975, Archbishop of Westminster 1963–65. Heenan was the authority that granted Alfred permission to continue saying Mass in the old rite both publicly and privately, though limited to a congregation of no more than thirty, and not to be advertised on church billboards as a regular occurrence]. In [an] earlier [letter] he had stated his intention of retiring in the summer of 1966. That letter had, however, been written "in belief that no change would take place in the nature of the Chaplaincy or consequently in the composition of the Cambridge University Catholic Association or the Fisher Society until after my retirement." Successive meetings of the Fisher Society Committee and the CUCA Council had, however, convinced him that they were determined to act independently of the Chaplain. "The issue which has caused me to advance the date of my retirement [to December 17, 1965] is not," he wrote, "one of admission of women or clergy to this society or that. It is, rather, one of authority or (in military language) of a chain of command. I am convinced that not only I, but no other priest would willingly hold a position in which the general policy of the Chaplaincy and the affairs of the undergraduate society were alike outside his control. The authority of the Chaplain is derived from the Bishops through the Board (which is the instrument of the hierarchy), and the general responsibility of the Chaplaincy must be his. The purposes of the CUCA and the Fisher Society can be achieved only by their working in harmony with him. The policy of the Chaplaincy can be controlled from above by the Hierarchy acting through the Board. It should not be subject to pressure from below.'" Peter Gregory-Jones, *A History of the Cambridge Catholic Chaplaincy, 1895–1965*.

13. Regarding Alfred's attitude to women in general, one reviewer of David Watkin's collection of essays about him remarks: 'There is ... a touch of "protest too much" on the question of misogyny. The argument against might have been more convincing if the 13 contributors had included, say, a couple of women—Glenys Roberts (who published Gilbey's Commonplace Book), for instance, or perhaps even a wife of one of the married men in the Monsignor's "flock"'. (Hugh Massingberd, 'The eccentricities of Monsignor Gilbey', review of *Alfred Gilbey: A Memoir by Some Friends*, David Watkin, *Spectator* March 16, 2002). As one of his closest friends said of him: 'It could seem almost provocatively convenient for a man clearly more emotionally comfortable with members of his own sex so confidently to champion all-male institutions.' (Nicholas Lorriman in *Alfred Gilbey: A Memoir by Some Friends*, 105). In fairness one should point out that the selection of contributors to the book was almost certainly made by the editor, and that many women found Alfred both charming and *sympatico*.

14. Permission for undergraduates to share rooms with their girlfriends—or girls with their boyfriends, and presumably partners in same-sex couples—had in fact already been granted at Cambridge some time before my interview with Alfred. His own dear Trinity had permitted such arrangements since 1992. When I went up to Peterhouse, by contrast, in 1984 (still then an almost all-male college, but for the first four female undergraduates admitted that year), the rules forbade women to stay the night in a man's room, though they allowed men to.

15. I was unable to source this attribution. Perhaps it referred to the Episcopalian bishop John Shelby Spong (1931–2021), who had written a

book called *Living in Sin?: A Bishop Rethinks Human Sexuality* (1988). The Episcopal Church in the United States is a member church of the worldwide Anglican communion.

16. The reader may wonder, if Alfred was right, how on earth Oxford managed with a co-ed chaplaincy from the middle of the Second World War onwards!

17. The reader may be surprised to find Alfred here apparently defending gay rights. In spite of these comments, he always upheld the Church's teaching that the only sinless sex was that between a man and a woman within the sacrament of marriage.

18. There is some scientific evidence to support Alfred's view. See T. David-Barrett, *Women Favour Dyadic Relationships, but Men Prefer Clubs: Cross-Cultural Evidence from Social Networking*, National Library of Medicine, March 16, 2015, //www.ncbi.nlm.nih.gov/pmc/articles/PMC4361571/

19. William Whiteley (1831–1907), English entrepreneur of the late 19th and early 20th centuries. Founder of the William Whiteley Limited retail company whose eponymous department store became the Whiteleys shopping centre.

20. The Chesterton quotation comes from Maisie Ward, *Gilbert Keith Chesterton* (New York: Sheed & Ward, 1944). Extract quoted in Alfred Gilbey, *The Commonplace Book of Monsignor Gilbey*, Glenys Roberts, ed., (London: Bellew Publishing Company Ltd, 1993). Cf. George Eliot (1819–1880): 'I should like to know what is the proper function of women, if it is not to make reasons for husbands to stay at home, and still stronger reasons for bachelors to go out.' *The Mill on the Floss*, book VI, ch. 6, (1860).

21. Gilbey, *We Believe*, Chapter 19, 'The Fourth and Fifth Commandments', 216–217.

22. For the 'guying' by Fr Incledon to which Alfred refers, see Appendix II: *Alfred Against the Liberals*.

23. Gilbey, *We Believe*, Chapter 19, 'The Fourth and Fifth Commandments', 216.

24. Alfred's examples of three saints with widely differing vocations within their contrasting states of life are: St Louis of France (King Louis IX, 1214–70, reigned 1226–70), who entertained St Thomas Aquinas to dinner; St Thomas More (1478–1535), Lord Chancellor of England, author of *Utopia* and martyr under Henry VIII, and St Benedict Joseph Labré (1748–83), confessor. Labré, a member of the Third Order of St Francis, was a lifelong wandering mendicant pilgrim who settled in Rome in 1774, sleeping rough in the Colosseum. He would not have agreed with John

Wesley, the Methodist founder, that 'cleanliness is next to godliness.' Labré is patron saint, among other things, of beggars, tramps, the homeless, and mentally ill people.

25. St Benedict (c. 480–c. 550), Abbot and Founder of Subiaco and Monte Casino Abbeys, author of the *Rule* which bears his name, Patriarch of Western Monasticism, patron of Europe. The impact of his *Rule* and of the monks who followed it had extraordinarily powerful and pervasive effects on the development of Catholic culture over the centuries. Arguably more so than any other person, St Benedict can lay claim to being the cornerstone of Catholic civilisation in Western Europe.

26. This description of St Philip Neri (1515–95) could be applied equally well to Alfred, of whom Fr Ronald Creighton-Jobe of the London Oratory wrote 'his own brand of asceticism was to be always available to those who sought him, no matter how demanding they might be.' Ronald Creighton-Jobe in *Alfred Gilbey: A Memoir by Some Friends*, 25. St Philip, priest, founder of the Congregation of the Oratory (which St John Henry Newman [1801–90] and Frederick William Faber, [1814–1863], introduced to England), was known as the Apostle of Rome. Newman wrote of him: 'St Philip lived in an age as traitorous to the interests of Catholicism as any that preceded it, or can follow it. He saw the great and gifted, dazzled by the Enchantress; he saw heathen forms mounting; all this he saw, and he perceived that the mischief was to be met, not with argument, not with science, not with protests and warnings, not by the recluse or the preacher, but by means of the great counter-fascination of purity and truth.' *The Idea of a University Defined and Illustrated*, 1873.

27. Gilbey, *We Believe*, Chapter 19, 'The Fourth and Fifth Commandments', 218–219.

28. The *Collegio Ecclesiastico Beda*, a seminary at Rome, founded in 1852, principally then to provide for Anglican converts from the Oxford Movement, other convert clergy and late vocations; refounded 1898 and still going strong. Unfortunately, no record exists at the college of Alfred's dates there. One must assume c. 1924–29, as he graduated from Cambridge in 1924, and was ordained in 1929.

29. In his 1990 interview with Naim Atallah, Alfred said: 'A book that had a great influence on me was *Hugh*, A. C. Benson's memoir of his younger brother R. H. Benson. There were three brothers, the sons of the Archbishop of Canterbury at the beginning of the century, all of whom were prolific writers, though Hugh was the only one who became a Catholic and a priest. He was an immensely dynamic character, writing and preaching ceaselessly, a great convert maker, and it fell to me as a little boy at Beaumont to read what his brother had written about him.

This presentation of a priest was so different from any I had known that I asked one of the Jesuits how it was that Hugh Benson was, as a priest, able to lead the life depicted. The Jesuit explained that he was a secular, and this was the first time I ever heard of the existence of the secular clergy.' Naim Atallah, *Singular Encounters* (London: Quartet Books, 1991).

R. H. Benson, 1871–1914; ordained C of E 1895; converted to Rome 1903. Most of his prolific literary output is Catholic apologia. Novels include *Come Rack! Come Rope!*, *The Average Man* and *The Lord of the World*. E. F. Benson (1867–1940) was best known for his Mapp and Lucia novels. A. C. Benson (1862–1925) wrote the lyrics of Land of Hope and Glory (1902).

Beaumont College (1861–1967) was a public school in Old Windsor, Berkshire. Founded and run by the Society of Jesus, it was, like the nearby Eton College, within easy reach of London, and therefore preferred by many families to the longer-established Jesuit foundation Stonyhurst College in Lancashire.

30. Edward Cuthbert Butler (1858–1934), *Benedictine Monachism: Studies in Benedictine Life and Rule* (London: Longmans Green, 1919). Butler was Abbot of Downside 1906–22, when he resigned. He was an ecclesiastical historian. Butler is best known for *The Vatican Council: The Story from Inside in Bishop Ullathorne's Letters*. He also wrote on mysticism.

31. This was in the days before mobile phones.

32. This reference to the Victorian father may hold true for regulation of literature admitted to the household, but in terms of what the same man would have seen on the streets of London, there would have been a great many prostitutes soliciting in certain areas. Nonetheless, by the standards of modern prostitutes—and, indeed, of many modern women who are not prostitutes—their manner of dress would have been relatively very modest.

33. Stonyhurst College, the Jesuit-founded boarding school in Lancashire, originally for boys, now co-ed and principally lay-run, founded 1794.

34. My emphasis, lest an inattentive reader fall for the contention of Canon Incledon (Alfred's successor as Chaplain) in his review of *We Believe* that Alfred 'dismisses attempts to build the Kingdom of God on earth'. What he really means, no doubt, is that Alfred implicitly dismisses *socialist* attempts to do so. Nonetheless, I am most grateful to the late Canon Incledon (1929–2012) for his eminently kind and courteous help with my inquiries. I note also that he took up the saying of Mass in the old rite. He was Chaplain at Cambridge from 1966–77.

35. ... 'in no circumstances commit sin to achieve or preserve [material well-being].' Nonetheless, the Church has traditionally taught the following: 'The seventh commandment forbids *theft*, that is, usurping another's property against the reasonable will of the owner. There is no theft if consent can be presumed or if refusal is contrary to reason and the universal destination of goods. This is the case in obvious and urgent necessity when the only way to provide for immediate, essential needs (food, shelter, clothing ...) is to put at one's disposal and use the property of others.' *Catechism of the Catholic Church*, section 2408 (Geoffrey Chapman Ltd., 1994), 514–515.

36. Gilbey, *We Believe*, Chapter 21, 'The Seventh, Tenth and Eighth Commandments', 234.

37. Gilbey, We Believe, Chapter 1, 'The Foundation of Faith in Reason', 19.

38. For readers unfamiliar with the terminology of the Penny Catechism: 'The seven Corporal Works of Mercy are: 1. To feed the hungry. 2. To give drink to the thirsty. 3. To clothe the naked. 4. To harbour the harbourless. 5. To visit the sick. 6. To visit the imprisoned. 7. To bury the dead... The seven Spiritual Works of Mercy are: 1. To convert the sinner. 2. To instruct the ignorant. 3. To counsel the doubtful. 4. To comfort the sorrowful. 5. To bear wrongs patiently. 6. To forgive injuries. 7. To pray for the living and the dead.' *The Catechism of Christian Doctrine approved by the Archbishops and Bishops of England and Wales* (London: The Catholic Truth Society, 1971). (The edition on which *We Believe* is based).

39. Mother Teresa (1910–1997), founder of the Missionaries of Charity, died just over six months before Alfred. She was canonised by Pope Francis in 2016, feast day is September 5.

40. I was unable to find online the statements which I remember having read about at the time. The following quotations come closest: 'I find poverty in a rich country more difficult to remove than poverty in a poor country,' ... 'Food aid can be gotten for a famine, but food for these people?' ... 'I never give a child for adoption to a family that uses contraceptives that kill the power of love,' ... 'How can a mother love another's child if she has killed the child of her love?', Graham Heathcote, 'Mother Teresa Weeps for London's Homeless' in *AP News*, April 14, 1988. Also: 'You in the West have the spiritually poorest of the poor much more than you have the physically poor. Often among the rich are very spiritually poor people. I find it is easy to give a plate of rice to a hungry person, to furnish a bed to a person who has no bed, but to console or to remove the bitterness, anger, and loneliness that comes from being spiritually

deprived, that takes a long time.' Becky Benenate, *Mother Teresa, Mother Teresa*, Joseph Durepos, ed. Source: https://www.spiritualityandpractice.com/quotes/quotations/view/10095/spiritual-quotation

41. María Eva Duarte de Perón, known as Eva Peron, (1919–1952), politician, activist, actress, and philanthropist who served as First Lady of Argentina from June 1946 until her death in July 1952, as the wife of Argentine President Juan Domingo Peron (1895–1974).

42. This line from the musical is somewhat misleading. In fact Eva Peron established the Fundacion Eva Peron with 10,000 pesos she donated. It did rely on direct state support but also on donations from the labour unions, which were obliged by law to contribute, and from businesses and individuals.

43. Fr Herbert McCabe OP (1926–2001), priest, major theologian and philosopher. Editor of *New Blackfriars*, 1965–67.

44. Maurice Couve de Murville (1929–2007), Chaplain at Cambridge 1977–82, Archbishop of Birmingham, 1982–99.

45. 'In 1980, a *Sunday Times* investigation revealed that in 1978, the Dewhurst chain paid £10 [sic] tax on a profit of more than £2.3m. By this time, Edmund's grandson, also Edmund, and his cousin, Lord Samuel, were at the helm. In an infamous remark the Tory grandee Lord Thorneycroft remarked: "Good luck to them."' Anonymous, 'Heirs and Disgraces', *The Guardian*, August 11, 1999, additional research by Sally Narraway.

46. *The Catechism of the Catholic Church* teaches: "Submission to authority and co-responsibility for the common good make it morally obligatory to pay taxes..." (No. 2240). 'It is a moral obligation for citizens to pay their fair share of taxes for the common good, including the good of poor and vulnerable communities, just as states also have an obligation to provide "a reasonable and fair application of taxes" with "precision and integrity in administering and distributing public resources."' (Compendium of the Social Doctrine of the Church, No. 355). Paul L Caron, Tax Prof Blog, Caruso School of Law, September 10, 2017. https://taxprof.typepad.com/taxprof_blog/2017/09/bainbridge-is-tax-avoidance-immoral-a-catholic-perspective.html

47. Alfred's defence of Lord Vestey and co. seems very legalistic. But he himself had no qualms about breaking the law when he smuggled money out of England: 'At Easter 1969 we made a memorable visit to Spain with Alastair Langlands, staying with Alfred's colourful relatives in Jerez de la Frontera. At the time, the Labour government had an extraordinarily repressive financial regime which limited the amount of British currency one could take abroad to an absurd sum like fifty or a hundred pounds

[Actually £50 plus £15 in sterling cash. The purpose was to prevent a run on the pound. These controls had originally been brought in at various levels at the start of the War in 1939. They were abolished by Margaret Thatcher's government in 1979]. I remember the astonishment with which Alastair and I found, as soon as we had been through the passport control at the airport, that Alfred's clothes were stuffed with hundreds of pounds' worth of bank notes.' Watkin, ed., *Alfred Gilbey: A Memoir by Some Friends*, 124. In quoting this I don't mean to condemn Alfred for apparent double standards regarding the law, merely to show that he was not always as legalistic as his comments on the McCabe catechism might make him appear. The law he broke in 1969 was clearly either 'absurd' in principle, as David Watkin implies, or at the very least absurdly restrictive in the limit, even if debatably justified in principle.

48. Gilbey, *We Believe*, Chapter 21, 'The Seventh, Tenth and Eighth Commandments', 232–233.

49. Gilbey, *We Believe*, Chapter 1, 'The Foundation of Faith in Reason', 13.

50. Alfred's opinion should be set against the spate of revelations of sexual abuse by clergy in the Catholic Church, many of which go back decades and were covered up by those in the hierarchy.

51. In the period Alfred describes, consequent upon the Matrimonial Causes Act of 1857, a husband's grounds for divorce needed only be adultery alone, while a wife had to prove both adultery and one of the following: bigamy, incest, desertion, cruelty, sodomy or bestiality. In spite of the censorship applying to other spheres of publication, all of these could be mentioned, sometimes in detail, in the press. 'Following the Judicial Proceedings (Regulation of Reports) Act 1926, journalists could only report case judgements, but in Argyll v Argyll, this was damning enough. The judgement took over three hours to read and it eviscerated Margaret Campbell's character. Branded the "Dirty Duchess" by the press, this misogynistic moniker continues to be used nearly 60 years later.' Dr Jennifer Aston, Senior Lecturer in History at Northumbria University, 'EXPERT COMMENT: A Very British Scandal: divorce courts have been shaming women since the 1800s', Press Release of January 19, 2022. https://newsroom.northumbria.ac.uk/pressreleases/expert-comment-a-very-british-scandal-divorce-courts-have-been-shaming-women-since-the-1800s-3156137. In the words of the 1926 Act: 'It shall not be lawful to print or publish, or cause or procure to be printed or published… in relation to any judicial proceedings any indecent matter or indecent medical, surgical or physiological details being matters or details the publication of which would be calculated to injure public morals.' It sounds as if Queen Mary (wife of George V, who reigned 1910–36) got her way!

52. The rule forbidding divorced people to use the Royal Enclosure was abolished in 1962. Had it not been, the Queen's sister Princess Margaret would eventually have been barred. She divorced Lord Snowdon in 1978.

53. 'Whosoever putteth away his wife, and marrieth another, committeth adultery: and whosoever marrieth her that is put away from her husband committeth adultery.' Luke 16:18.

54. The French Colonel was Lieut. Col. Jacques Balsan. He had been decorated with the Legion d'Honneur (the highest French military or civil medal) for exceptional service rendered to the Ministry of War as an officer in the First World War. A flying pioneer and ballooning height record-breaker (in 1900), he had commanded a squadron during the war. In 1918, he went to London as chief of the French Air Force mission. He had been in love with the duchess before she married the duke, from his first sight of her when she was 17. She married the duke when she was 17 or 18.

55. The 'novelette' to which Alfred refers is *The Glitter and the Gold*, ghost-written for the duchess, Consuelo Vanderbilt Balsan, Heinemann, 1953; second edition St Martin's Press 2012. The 'glitter' symbolised the superficial attraction of her marriage to the duke, the 'gold', her true love-match with Balsan. The author says that she approached the Roman Rota in 1926, so it was not in fact until some 27 years later — not the three that Alfred thought — that she wrote down her account of the affair. For the relevant extract see my Appendix III: The Marlborough Annulment. Though mainly launched as a way to facilitate the Anglican duke's wish to convert to Catholicism, the annulment was also fully supported by the former duchess's mother, who testified: "I forced my daughter to marry the duke", adding: "I have always had absolute power over my daughter." In later years, Consuelo and her mother had a warmer, easier relationship. This seems to contradict Alfred's assertion that the annulment was the duchess's project. But perhaps both accounts are right: it served the proper interests of both parties. In the duchess's own words: 'Sanctified as our marriage [that with Balsan] had been in an Episcopal church, it was to me completely valid; and I would have been content to ignore the ultra-religious views that prevented the orthodox Catholics from recognising it. But in 1926, when Marlborough decided he wanted his first marriage annulled, the pressure brought by my French family and my desire to see Jacques at peace with them determined my decision to approach the Rota.'

56. 'As I have already said, there are but two alternatives, the way to Rome, and the way to Atheism: Anglicanism is the halfway house on the one side, and Liberalism is the halfway house on the other. How many men were there, as I knew full well, who would not follow me

now in my advance from Anglicanism to Rome, but would at once leave Anglicanism and me for the Liberal camp. It is not at all easy (humanly speaking) to wind up an Englishman to a dogmatic level. I had done so in good measure, in the case both of young men and of laymen, the Anglican *Via Media* being the representative of dogma. The dogmatic and the Anglican principle were one, as I had taught them; but I was breaking the *Via Media* to pieces, and would not dogmatic faith altogether be broken up, in the minds of a great number, by the demolition of the *Via Media*? Oh! How unhappy this made me!' (St John Henry Newman, *Apologia Pro Vita Sua*, Chapter 4, 'History of My Religious Opinions from 1841 to 1845', 137.)

57. Gilbey, *We Believe*, Chapter 1, 'The Foundation of Faith in Reason', 18.

58. 'The 1993 Education Act included some new challenges for sex education. It stated that only the biological aspects of HIV, AIDS, STIs and human sexual behaviour could be included in the National Curriculum. Parents were also given the right to withdraw their children from sex education and were not required to give a reason.' https://www.sexeducationforum.org.uk/about/our-history-30-years-campaigning

59. This statement of Alfred's needs to be put into its dogmatic context: '496. What is the meaning of the conjugal act? The conjugal act has a twofold meaning: unitive (the mutual self-giving of the spouses) and procreative (an openness to the transmission of life). No one may break the inseparable connection which God has established between these two meanings of the conjugal act by excluding one or the other of them.' *Compendium of the Catechism of the Catholic Church*, 145. The point to be taken is that, in his emphasis on the procreative, Alfred seems to have forgotten to include the unitive meaning. See also the following paragraph from the Compendium: '497. When is it moral to regulate births? The regulation of births, which is an aspect of responsible fatherhood and motherhood, is objectively morally acceptable when it is pursued by the spouses without external pressure; when it is practised not out of selfishness but for serious reasons; and with methods that conform to the objective criteria of morality, that is, periodic continence and use of the infertile periods.' *Compendium of the Catechism of the Catholic Church* (London: The Incorporated Catholic Truth Society, 2006), 145. Ergo the conjugal act is still good, holy and honourable even when it is not intended to be procreative, provided the foregoing conditions are met.

60. Alfred is referring to the UN International Conference on Population and Development (ICPD), held at Cairo in September 1994. This was marked by controversy between the Holy See and the richer nations arising from the former's defence, in solidarity with many of

the developing, and all the Muslim, countries, against both the proposal to establish abortion as a legal right and for coercive birth control, and against foreign aid being made conditional on the acceptance of birth control programmes. On paper those aligned with the Holy See's position appeared to have won the day in resisting the unwanted proposals, in the sense that an agreement was reached giving states the sovereign right to exclude abortion from their legislation. But at the UN Earth Summit in New York (June 1997), attempts by the European Union to overrule the agreement were made. In spite of these efforts, wording upholding the national sovereignty of countries in determining their own legislation was then reaffirmed. However, more recently, on July 6, 2022, MEPs voted successfully for abortion 'rights' to be included in the EU Charter of Fundamental Rights. 324 voted in favour, 155 against, with 38 abstentions. The resolution condemned the US Supreme Court decision to overturn federal abortion rights. (Source: Sara-Taissir Bencharif, https://www.politico.eu/article/meps-vote-for-abortion-rights-to-be-in-eu-charter-of-fundamental-rights/ *Politico*, July 7, 2022.)

61. Gilbey, *We Believe*, Chapter 20, 'The Sixth and Ninth Commandments', 227.

62. *Humanae Vitae*, 19 (London: Incorporated Catholic Truth Society, 1968). See Appendix IV: '*Humanae Vitae*: Pope Paul's Prophetic Words'.

63. Gerard Manley Hopkins, 'To What Serves Mortal Beauty?' Hopkins (1844–89) was a convert and Jesuit much influenced by Newman and the Oxford Movement while an undergraduate at Oxford. The poem begins: 'To what serves mortal beauty? — dangerous; does set danc-/ing blood — '. Gerard Manley Hopkins, *Selected Poetry* (Oxford: Oxford University Press 2008).

64. 'And God blessed them, saying: Increase and multiply, and fill the earth, and subdue it, and rule over the fishes of the sea, and the fowls of the air, and all living creatures that move upon the earth' (Genesis 1:28, DRC).

65. See Appendix V: *Church Teaching and World Population: God's Truth and A Persistent Myth*. This is a critique of certain false beliefs about world population.

66. Gilbey, *We Believe*, Chapter 16, 'The Sacrament of Penance', 179.

67. 'And he gave some apostles, and some prophets, and other some evangelists, and other some pastors and doctors' (Ephesians 4:11, DRC).

68. I find Alfred's answer to this question (whether a Christian should belong to a socially exclusive club) quite hard to take. Can a proper parallel really be made between the class distinctions that deny most people the

possibility of election to a 'gentlemen's' club and those between the various vocations to which the Holy Spirit calls people, the special status of the Jewish people as God's chosen race, or the exclusive vision of the Transfiguration to three of the Apostles? Perhaps so. But the vehemence of his reaction is telling. I had touched his anti-egalitarian nerve. In his defence, one could say that the very fact that Our Lord would have been blackballed from the Travellers meant that it was necessary for Alfred to smuggle Him in, as he did by saying Mass in the club and reserving the Blessed Sacrament in his tiny chapel, as by acting *in persona Christi* to all he met.

I observe that Alfred's great loathing of egalitarianism expressed itself sometimes in questionable ways. When I told him that his exact Cambridge contemporary, the Bloomsbury diarist Frances Partridge (1900–2004) objected to her father's omission of a bathroom in his new maidservants' quarters, he said dismissively 'Of course, she was an egalitarian'. I could not help feeling that wanting a tired and sweaty servant to be able to have a bath after a day's hard work is not exactly a Bolshevik notion. It might even be thought of as charitable, or Christian!

Incidentally, Alfred told me that none of his Cambridge contemporaries were still alive. Partridge was, but being a woman, she didn't feature on his radar. Technically, of course, in Alfred's clear distinction, she was not a fellow undergraduate, but a mere 'student', as women could not take university degrees at Cambridge until 1948. In another interview (with Naim Atallah, businessman, writer and publisher, 1931–2021), Alfred had said he did not meet any women in his four years as an undergraduate at Cambridge.

69. *Frances Partridge*, Naim Atallah Online, an interview with Naim Atallah, posted August 15, 2014, https://quartetbooks.wordpress.com/2014/08/15/frances-partridge/.

70. 'The next Pope but five' from Pius XI was in fact Benedict XVI, who, as a German, had obviously not been a member of the Ballila, though he had been, as was compulsory, a member of the Hitler Youth (though one who later risked his life by deserting). But the next Pope but three, John Paul I (1912–78, in office August 26–September 28, 1978, who only lasted just over a month before he died), would have been in the Mussolini Youth as a lad. If so, the propaganda to which he was subjected left no trace of sympathy with Fascism. '... his family were known as outspoken socialists... In 1949... he had a good working relationship with local Communists... [later] he moved unobtrusively to the right politically, declaring publicly (at the election of June 1975) that Communism was incompatible with Christianity... [But]... he had no use for ecclesiastical display, encouraged parish priests to sell precious vessels and other church valuables for the benefit of the poor, and in 1971 proposed that the wealthy

churches of the West should give one percent of their income to the impoverished churches of the third world... Always impatient of pomp and outward trappings, and transparently humble-minded, he dispensed with the traditional papal coronation...' J. N. D. Kelly, *The Oxford Dictionary of Popes* (Oxford: Oxford University Press, 1986), 325–326.

71. Gilbey, *We Believe*, 'Fundamentals and Accidentals', 247–249.

72. 'Truth alone is worthy of our entire devotion.' This is the epigraph to *We Believe*, a quotation from the great and saintly Irish Dominican friar, scholar and evangelist Fr Vincent McNabb (1868–1943).

73. 'We hold these truths to be self-evident, that all men are endowed by their Creator with certain fundamental rights, that among these are life, liberty and the pursuit of happiness.' The American Declaration of Independence, July 4, 1776.

74. Cf. Pope Paul VI in *Humanae Vitae*: 'Man cannot attain that true happiness for which he yearns with all the strength of his spirit, unless he keeps the laws which the Most High God has engraved in his very nature.'

75. '1. Who made you? God made me. 2. Why did God make you? God made me to know him, love him and serve him in this world, and to be happy with him forever in the next.' *The Catechism of Christian Doctrine approved by the Archbishops and Bishops of England and Wales*, 3.

APPENDIX I
Alfred and Franco

TO PUT IN PERSPECTIVE ALFRED'S REFERENCE to the 'so-called refugees' from Franco, and his warm support for Franco's government, the following facts should be considered:

1. Had Franco lost the Civil War (July 18, 1936–April 1, 1939), the atheistic government of the leftist Popular Front would likely have continued unchecked in its ruthless persecution of the Church, or where it was not directly responsible for persecution, in continuing to turn a blind eye to that meted out by its more extreme and anarchist allies. This had included:

> a) the burning down of churches and convents;
> b) the wholesale slaughter of bishops, priests, monks and nuns: respectively twelve, 5,255, 283 and 249;
> c) atrocities such as the forcing of Rosary beads into the ears of nuns and playing football with their skulls.

2. '"Francoism"' was not a distinctive ideology. Franco stood for traditional Catholic and military values and was an implacable enemy of liberal, left-wing and separatist forces. Francoism as a term is mainly used to refer to Franco's regime. Although this had some features of fascism, and its creation relied upon military support from Hitler, ... and Mussolini, the regime was authoritarian rather than totalitarian.' Iain McLean and Alistair McMillan, *The Concise Oxford Dictionary of Politics* (Oxford: Oxford University Press 1996), 205.

Although it is true that Franco was glad to have the military assistance of the Luftwaffe and the fascist Italian *Aviazione Legionara* to bomb his enemy, as iconically attested in Picasso's *Guernica*, it should be noted that Guernica was then being used as a communications centre by Republican forces. The raid was meant to destroy bridges and roads, but it also had the declared intent of demoralising enemy forces and their civilian supporters, who were gathered in large numbers for market day, through sheer terror. It helped enable Franco's capture of Bilbao and victory in Northern Spain. If Franco was wrong to ally with Hitler, then by the same token the Allies were wrong to enlist Stalin's military help in the Second World War. Without Hitler's and Mussolini's assistance, the Civil War would have dragged on, with yet more lives being lost. It is nonetheless true that some 50,000 Republicans were executed after the war in recrimination against the former enemy. Perhaps Franco saw this as a necessary pre-emptive strike against potential future revolutionaries, perhaps he saw it as just punishment, perhaps both.

3. For Alfred's critique of democracy, which implies a strong inclination to prefer authoritarian government, one need only read his words in the first appendix of *We Believe*:

> We now expect to have things "as we like". It is part of the backwash of democracy that people should have the government they like, the legislation they like, the education they like. This pervasive tendency is powerfully played upon by advertising, mass media, market research and the rest. The housewife must have the goods she likes in the packet she likes. Our likes, which are the most irrational, the most irresponsible, the most fitful part of our being are elevated into a principle. Fashion, which is the collective like of a period, is canonised. Departure from fashion becomes reprehensible.' (Gilbey, *We Believe*, 'Fundamentals and Accidentals', 246.)

One might object that it would not have been a matter of fashionable preference, but a stern obligation of moral duty to care for those dismissed by Alfred as 'the so-called refugees from Franco', not all of whom can have been guilty of sacrilegious and murderous atrocities, even if many had fought for a side that had committed them. In fact, given Franco's policy of capital punishment of prisoners of war, they would have had what the Home Office nowadays calls a 'well-founded fear of persecution'. It is also true that there were many atrocities on Franco's side.

But to summarise the situation as it appeared to many Catholics at the time, the Italian Archbishop of Gorizia wrote in 1939, the last year of the Civil War: 'Good Italians (and today we are entitled to believe that in the Fascist climate all Italians are worthy

Appendix I

of their name) know that in Red Spain all the worst elements of the sinister democratic regimes have united to make a final effort against the granite mass of Christian civilisation.'

To put things in perspective, I ask the reader to ponder the following account, in an extended extract from an impartial historian:

> In spite of the claims of contemporaries and Republican propaganda, neither the Church nor Pius XI can justly be accused of provoking a quarrel with left wing forces in Spain. By 1930 the military regime of Primo de Rivera, which had been supported by the Church, came to an end. This regime had been corrupt, and was increasingly rejected by the rising middle classes. With the resignation of Rivera, the Monarchists were defenceless, King Alphonso XIII abdicated and in April 1931 a republic was proclaimed under the leadership of Niceto Alcala Zamora. The new Socialist Government abrogated the Concordat and separated Church and State, confiscated ecclesiastical property and expelled the Jesuits, secularised education and introduced divorce, abolished clerical privileges and prohibited religious processions; "with these measures" declared the Prime Minister, "Spain ceases to be Catholic."
>
> The adoption of anticlerical provisions and total disestablishment in the Spanish Constitution of 1931 has been described by a recent historian of the Spanish Civil War as 'political folly.' Spanish Catholics had 'to oppose the very Constitution of the Republic if they wished to criticise its educational or religious policy.' Nevertheless the end of the Monarchy and the proclamation of the Republic were not originally opposed by Spanish Catholics. The Republic did not immediately enforce its anti-clerical measures and several bishops urged their people to accept the Republic as the lawful government. Bishops and Catholic activists welcomed the new regime and the *Te Deum* was even sung in thanksgiving. The initial reaction of the Holy See was also restrained. The Papal Nuncio was instructed to establish good relations with the Republicans even before they came to power and this he had done. He was able to have several friendly conversations with representatives of the Government which at least originally showed its respect for the Church. When Cardinal Segura, the Archbishop of

Toledo and Primate of Spain, an intransigent Monarchist, condemned the new Republic and was sent into exile, the Vatican authorities were clearly embarrassed. In due course he resigned as Primate and joined the Roman curia.

The Socialist Government, however, proved incapable of controlling its more extreme and anarchist allies who plundered and destroyed churches, monasteries and convents all over Spain. In 1933 [the second year of Alfred's Chaplaincy at Cambridge] the Pope [Pius XI] demanded religious freedom and protested against the violence to which the Church was being subjected in an encyclical, *Dilectissima Nobis*, but again did not attack the Spanish Republic. As political opinion began to polarise and left-wing elements began to attack the Church and the clergy, Spanish Catholics rallied to the defence of their religion. The moderation of the Holy See encouraged the emergence of a new Catholic Republican party led by Jose Maria Gil Robles. The Socialists lost their majority in elections held during 1933 and the new Catholic party was the largest of the right-wing parties which gained control. Negotiations were started with a view to signing a new Concordat and compensation was paid to those clergy who had lost their benefices as a result of the anti-clerical legislation passed in 1931.

The General Election in 1936 was expected to return the right-wing parties to power but although these gained several hundred thousand more votes than their left-wing opponents, there was a sizable left wing majority in the Spanish Cortes. The Popular Front included Communists and Anarchists as well as Republicans and Socialists. A political amnesty released thousands more Anarchists as well as common criminals, and within days there were further outbursts of anti-clericalism. The attacks on churches and religious houses, accompanied with murders and arson, began all over again. Priests and religious were physically attacked and five nuns were lynched. The murder of Calvo Sotelo, a monarchist deputy who had protested in the Cortes against the toleration extended to murderers and arsonists, precipitated the Civil War. A number of regiments in Spanish Morocco mutinied and General Francisco Franco flew there to raise the standard of the Falange [a fascist organisation founded as the Falange Espanola in 1933 by Jose Antonio Primo de Rivera ...Through its manifesto adopted in 1934, the Twenty-Seven Points, it espoused political illiberalism and authoritarianism, and a belief in national community devoid of class conflict, nationalism, and hostility to other ideologies or intellectual discussion. Through paternalistic social values it successfully enlisted and reinforced the power of the Roman Catholic Church.'] Jan Palmowski, *A Dictionary of Twentieth-Century World History* (Oxford: Oxford University Press, 1997). Once the rebellion spread to the Spanish mainland, garrisons throughout Spain rose in sympathy.

Shortly after the outbreak of the Civil War, the Pope received a number of refugees, including bishops, priests and nuns as well as representatives of the laity. He bitterly condemned the persecution of the Church in Spain and gave his blessing: 'To all those who have assumed the difficult and dangerous task of defending and restoring the rights and honour of God and religion, which is to say the rights and dignity of conscience, the prime condition and the most solid basis for all human and civil welfare.'

At the same time he warned the refugees against indulging in selfish interests or party feelings and went on to describe as 'Our children' those who had murdered priests, destroyed churches and proscribed religion: 'We cannot doubt for a single instant what We have to do: to love them, to love them with a special love born of pity and compassion; to love them and, since We cannot do more, to pray for them; to pray that they may come back to the father who awaits them and for whom their return would be an occasion of the truest joy.'

Nevertheless, although there could be little doubt where the Pope's personal sympathies lay, Pius XI adopted a cautious line diplomatically. In spite of the murders of priests and religious, the confiscation of ecclesiastical property and the expulsion of the Jesuits, the official attitude of the Vatican remained conciliatory. On three occasions during the Civil War, Franco unsuccessfully tried to gain the recognition of the Vatican for his regime. However, the Holy See did not immediately join the German or Italian Governments when these recognised the Nationalist Government but continued to maintain formal, though very tenuous, contact with the administration in Madrid. The Holy See formally recognised the "Burgos authorities" as the official Spanish Government at the end of August 1937, though a full Nuncio was not sent until the end of 1938.

The Pope could not be unconscious of the fact that with the coming of the Civil War, the Falange had begun to demonstrate a religious fervour that had not been obvious before in either their ideology or their policies. The attitudes of Falangists were unpleasantly reminiscent of those of the Nazis or the [Italian] Fascists and the motives of all three groups were clearly something less than religious. The Holy See did not associate itself with the authoritarian aims of Franco or with the power politics of his German and Italian supporters. Pius XI did not welcome Franco's close relations with Mussolini and Hitler and he continuously insisted that his sole interest in the struggle was to free the Spanish Church from persecution. Furthermore he refused to condemn the Basques and even complained at the execution of some Basque priests by the Nationalists. But the Pope could hardly remain impassive in the face of the actual conduct of the war.

As left-wing attacks on the Church increased, the sympathies of the Vatican inevitably moved in favour of the Nationalists. Churches and religious buildings were savagely and deliberately destroyed and those which did survive were used as cinemas, store-houses or market-halls, arms dumps, or gun emplacements. The number of people killed included twelve bishops, 5,255 priests, 2,492 monks, 283 nuns and 249 novices. One priest was forced to go through a form of marriage with his housekeeper before both of them were shot. A bishop was led out to his execution naked in front of nuns. The skulls of nuns were used as footballs. A priest was stripped and scourged, crowned with thorns and then shot. Of course, the Nationalists were also guilty of murdering their opponents and their victims are said to have numbered 40,000.' J. Derek Holmes, *The Papacy in the Modern World, 1914–78,* (London: Burns & Oates 1981), 96–99.

It is worth pausing to consider how little-known this account of things is among the general public, even among the well-educated,

Appendix I 85

in the United Kingdom. The liberal humanist consensus is that the Spanish Civil War was a struggle between heroic freedom-fighter Republicans and unspeakably evil Fascist supporters of Franco. The truth is, as ever, more complex than the tabloid-style portrayal of either side as goodies or baddies.

In closing it should be noted that Alfred, alarmed by the spread of Communism through Cambridge in the 1930s co-founded there an anti-Communist dining club, the Strafford. It was named in honour of Cambridge-educated Thomas Wentworth, Earl of Strafford (1593–1641), Charles I's 'authoritarian and efficient' centralising minister, who was executed, ostensibly for treason, by an Act of Attainder passed by the House of Lords 'terrorized by a howling London mob... Strafford had nobly released Charles from his promise to protect him, and so the King signed the Bill, fearful for the safety of his wife and children in the popular anger — perhaps his greatest error. Strafford was beheaded at Tower Hill before a crowd of about 200,000 people.' This happened partly because 'the opposition really believed that Strafford was about to clamp a Catholic dictatorship on England with foreign help. Strafford would have been wise to seek refuge abroad, but the King guaranteed his protection, saying that Strafford "should not suffer in his person, honour or fortune." Pym impeached him and locked him in the Tower on November 11, 1640, accusing him of a series of non-treasonable acts which together, he claimed, constituted treason, including subverting the laws and planning to bring the King's Irish army over to England.' 'Though he agreed with the opposition on the necessity of preserving the balance of the constitution, when it came to a choice between increasing the king's power or the people's he was firmly on the side of the king. Arrogant, ruthless and awe-inspiring, he promoted the King's government, and his own fortune with the same managerial skills; along with Laud in London, he followed a policy in the North — and later in Ireland — known as "Thorough", or "Through", i.e., putting through the King's policies with the utmost efficiency. In the North, he spent the eleven years Personal Rule (1629–40)... enforcing law and order in the remotest corners, and generally using the powers of the centralising State to protect the weak from the strong: i.e., to enforce the Poor Law, regulate enclosures and relieve hunger.'

E. N. Williams, *The Penguin Dictionary of English and European History 1485–1789* (New York: Penguin Books 1980), 418–420. The Pym who impeached Strafford was John Pym (1584–1643), ... leading opponent of ... Charles I in the Long Parliament ... on the outbreak of the Civil War, he organised the war-effort of the Parliamentary side', 370.

Some of Alfred's fellow founder-members of the Strafford fought on Franco's side. Some fell. May they, and all those who were killed in action, or executed or murdered as a consequence, on either side, rest in peace.

4. Shortly before his 90th birthday Alfred was asked about his support for Franco by the barrister, dramatist and screenwriter John Mortimer:

> 'Mortimer: Are you against the French Revolution?
>
> Gilbey: Insofar as it popularised the misleading concept of egalitarianism, yes.
>
> Mortimer: But if you had a thoroughly evil father, wouldn't you defy him?
>
> Gilbey: But not murder him, you know.
>
> Mortimer: And if you were living in a criminal dictatorship, like Nazi Germany, wouldn't a violent revolution be justified?
>
> Gilbey: It never works. If you're born into a country, you're born into a going thing. If there's a revolution you never get to the end of it. I don't believe one man one vote is a sort of moral law.
>
> Mortimer: But you supported Franco. He started a revolution against the Spanish government.
>
> Gilbey: It was a government that didn't seem able to stop people from burning churches.
>
> Mortimer: So a revolution's all right if the government allows churches to be burned?
>
> He was silent then, and I felt a little ashamed of myself at having used a barrister's tactics to cross-examine the gentle Monsignor.' John Mortimer, 'The Monsignor at Ninety', *The Spectator* (July 6, 1996).

Regarding the church burnings, I invite the reader to ponder the following account:

Appendix I

> '... news of the rash of church burnings which took place in Madrid, Malaga, Seville, Cadiz and Alicante on May 11 [1931, one year before Alfred took up his post as Chaplain] did not pass [Franco] by. The attacks were carried out largely by Anarchists, provoked by the belief that the Church was at the heart of the most reactionary activities in Spain. Franco was probably unaware of allegations that the first fires were started with aviation spirit secured from Cuatro Vientos aerodrome by his brother Ramon. He cannot, however, have failed to learn of his brother's published statement that "I contemplated with joy those magnificent flames as the expression of a people which wanted to free itself from clerical obscurantism." In notes for his prospective memoirs, jotted down nearly thirty years after the event, Franco described the church burnings as the event which defined the Republic. That reflects not only his underlying Catholicism, but also the extent to which the Church and the Army were increasingly flung together as the self-perceived victims of Republican persecution.'
> Paul Preston, *Franco* (London: Fontana Press, 1993), 79–80.

5. Regarding Alfred's implication that a violent revolution would not have been justified even against Hitler, although he supported Franco's against the Republican Government in Spain, consider the following. Hitler's government, as is well-known, not only massacred Jews, Gypsies, gay people, and those considered mentally or physically 'defective', but also many priests and religious who dared to speak out against it. It did not burn churches, but its supporters sometimes burned synagogues. The wartime Pope, Pius XII, is slandered for failing to strongly criticise the Holocaust. Yet, apart from the fact that having observed the result of so doing, when the Dutch bishops in July 1942 made an outspoken attack on Nazi policy towards the Jews—that more Jews, including hundreds of Jewish Catholics, were rounded up and sent to their deaths—he decided that silence, short of a general denunciation of extermination on grounds of race in his broadcasts of 1942 and 1943, was the lesser evil, his actions show not only a courageous willingness to counter Nazism, but a generous use of Vatican accommodation to shelter Jews. In fact, he took the initiative to meet British agents at the Vatican, persuading them to take seriously the plans of German plotters who intended to

assassinate Hitler. He vouched for the plotters' anti-Nazi credentials. This was the key factor in London's 1940 agreement to back the plots. Source: Gerald Korson, 'How Pius XII was an "active conspirator" in three anti-Hitler plots', *Crux* (June 17, 2016).

Indeed the doctrine of just assassination of an evil government has a respectable Catholic pedigree. St Pius V (1504–72, reigned January 7, 1566–May 1, 1572) encouraged the violent overthrow of the heretic tyrant (to her Catholic subjects) Elizabeth I. In the words of a novelist of Catholic origin: 'Apply to the Jesuit theologian, Juam Mariana de Talavera, who will explain to you in what circumstances you may lawfully kill your king and whether you had better hand him his poison in a goblet or smear it for him on his robe or his saddlebow.' James Joyce, *A Portrait of the Artist as a Young Man* (London: Everyman, 1991).

If one feels shocked or surprised at Alfred's refusal to contemplate regime change in the case of Hitler, one should perhaps be equally shocked by Our Lord's attitude to the Roman occupation of Judea. But even so, there is an inconsistency or apparent double standard concerning Alfred's view of Franco, in that he supported the latter's revolution against the Republican government. For further information on Alfred's take on Hitler: 'His knowledge of the Spanish Civil War ... did much to explain his hostility to the British alliance with Stalin during the Second World War, again a policy scarcely questioned by the media. He told me how Ronald Knox had asked anxiously at the outbreak of war in 1939, "Do the Bishops say it's a just war?" Alfred, by contrast, indifferent as to the opinion of the Bishops on this topic, was opposed to our fighting the war at all.' Watkin, ed. *Alfred Gilbey: A Memoir by Some Friends*, 124.

6. Finally, the personal motive: 'Alfred's respect for Franco ... was rooted in memories of the Civil War when his mother would anxiously await news of the fate of her family and friends at the hands of the Communists. When I asked one of them ... for her reminiscences of the war, she spoke of the relief she had felt at the imminent arrival of Franco as "the forces of order". Alfred could also never forget that the entire British media in the 1930s supported the Communists and Republicans.' Watkin, ed. *Alfred Gilbey: A Memoir by Some Friends*, 124.

APPENDIX II
Alfred Against the Liberals

Given its premises, the work can seldom be faulted. Its defects are those of its model: effective defusing of Christianity's explosive power by distinguishing counsels from Commandments (keep the Decalogue, discount the Sermon on the Mount); a spiritual individualism, dismissing attempts to build the kingdom of God on earth, more reminiscent of Luther than of Innocent III; lack of any reference to Scripture as a real source for Faith and Christian nourishment (the Catechism's own "habit of adducing texts from Holy Scripture" is noted as a phenomenon calling for explanation).

Even in pre-conciliar terms, the image of the vine and the branches is pressed beyond what it will bear: "the complete identity between the Church and Jesus Christ Himself," "seeing her as a person, that person being Christ"—and very plainly not being you or me or any of the people of God (a concept nowhere in evidence). This Church is explicitly exempted from the need to refer to any criterion outside itself—a super-person always inappealably right. (For Church read Party, and we are indeed in 1984).' Fr Richard Incledon (Alfred's immediate successor as Chaplain), 'Firm Instructions', *Times Literary Supplement* (September 21, 1984).

Every one of Fr Incledon's charges is easily refuted simply by quoting *We Believe*. The idea that Alfred 'discounts the Sermon on the Mount': 'An individual who has no one dependent on him and is himself the subject of homicidal attack may either take the life of the assailant or turn the other cheek to the smiter, which is a very heroic thing to do.'; that he 'dismisses attempts to build the kingdom of God on earth': 'Poverty as popularly understood is destitution, ignorance, dirt and disease—the life of Shanty town. There is nothing Christian in that and we are urged not to cultivate it but to do what we can to eradicate it.'; that Alfred's work lacks 'any reference to Scripture as a real source for Faith and Christian nourishment': 'I would like you to turn now to St John 6: 27–67. This long passage, pointing forward to the Holy Eucharist, is very important and I want you to read it carefully several times. There are many things there for you to ponder.'; that he implies that the Church's identity with Christ excludes 'you or me or any of the people of God': 'If you want to understand at all what a Catholic means by the Church, remember one simple phrase which we have used before: the Church is Christ living on in His followers.'

As for Incledon's complaint that 'This Church is explicitly exempted from the need to refer to any criterion outside itself — a super-person always inappelably right', presumably Incledon has Holy Scripture in mind as the chief external criterion. Does he perhaps overlook Alfred's quote from the New Testament when it calls the Church 'the pillar and ground of truth'? (1 Timothy 3:15). Does Incledon forget that the main reason we are able to put our trust in the Church's teaching office as the living oracle of truth is that, as Our Lord Himself promised, the Holy Spirit guides her always, leading her into 'all truth' (John 16:13), and that, in the person of the Pope, He does so with particular care (Matthew 16:18). His mistake, it seems to me, like that of many critics of his ilk, has been to allow his distaste for certain aspects of Alfred's pre-conciliar style and approach to colour his judgement of the entire text. He has thrown out the Catholic baby with the Traditionalist bath-water.

Nonetheless, when Fr Incledon kindly sent me a copy of his review, he wrote at the bottom of the printed page: 'Presumably you know also that I was his successor at Cambridge, and can testify, with chapter and verse, to the personal courtesy, generosity and — I believe — even affection he displayed to somebody who differed so radically from himself and who dismantled so much of what he had built.' Incledon concluded his review with a remark which he must have hoped would be the *coup de grace* for Alfred's book. Referring to the essay 'Fundamentals and Accidentals', one of Alfred's appendixes, he says: 'This much-misunderstood essay plainly relativises those accidentals in the Church which are to the author's taste as much as those which are not. But has he not brought a Trojan horse into his own fortress? The whole scholastic rationalism which underlies the Catechism is a fashion of longer life — but still a fashion; the Faith can stand without it.'

To call the Church's scholastic tradition a fashion is daft. A philosophy superbly adapted to the exposition of Catholic doctrine which, beginning in the 9th century and still informing Catholic theologians today, among them the late St John Paul II, is not a fashion. It is a tradition. Indeed, in his words: 'Saint Thomas celebrates all the richness and complexity of each created being, and especially of the human being. It is not good that his thought has been set aside in the post-conciliar period; he continues, in fact, to be the *master of philosophical and theological universalism*. In this context, his *quinque viae* — that is, his 'five ways' that lead toward a response to the question '*An Deus sit*? [Does God exist?] — should be read.' St John Paul II, *Crossing the Threshold of Hope* (New York: Random House, London, 1995), 31.

So much for Incledon's critique. Alfred seems to have been unaware of an even less respectful review: 'The work clearly has the approval of the Peterhouse school of commentators on church, state and culture and has been more than welcomed by a number of disenchanted, not to say disaffected, Catholics whose disdain for today's Church is a prominent feature of their shared background and tastes.'

'There is no point in commenting on the bulk of the book, which, as one would expect, is as informative on Catholic teaching and practice as are very many other works now available to the public.' Talk of damning with faint praise! So wrote Fr Michael Richards, then editor of *The Clergy Review*, in *The Tablet* of May 5, 1984. A short list of some of the supposedly 'disenchanted, not to say disaffected' Catholics who 'more than welcomed' the book includes the one-time *papabile* Cardinal Hume; the then *papabile* Vatican-based Prefect Emeritus (as he now is) of the Congregation for Divine Worship, Cardinal Arinze; Archbishop Bruno Heim, formerly Apostolic Pro-Nuncio to the Court of St James, who in the *Osservatore Romano* of March 26, 1984 called it 'this timely book'; John Cardinal O'Connor, Archbishop of New York and Kevin McNamara, Archbishop of Dublin. The status and orthodoxy of these senior members of the hierarchy gives the lie to Fr Richards' absurd characterisation of *We Believe*.

Regarding Fr Incledon's 'guying' of the book, as Alfred described it, his successor wrote to me in a letter dated August 23, 1998: 'My reference, in the closing lines, to the last part of the book being "much misunderstood"... was in fact an oblique defence of Msgr Gilbey against what I thought was unfair criticism in other reviews, including *The Tablet*'s... It's sad to think that Alfred, from whom I received nothing but kindness and generosity, should feel that I "guyed" him. It certainly wasn't my intention. But he'll be clear about that now, God bless him. P. S. It was unfortunate that I ever accepted to do the review. My first instinct was to refuse, knowing how critical I was likely to be. Do you know the story of Cardinal Pole [1500–1558], drawing up a dignified letter of protest against Paul IV's paranoid attacks on him, and then destroying it, saying "Thou shalt not expose thy father's nakedness". I suppose I felt a bit like that.'

'But as it happened I already had the book at hand—it was originally published by subscription, and of course I had subscribed—so I took it up and opened it at random, and found a passage which made me say "Come, that's rather penetrating, I can do business with this." Only when I'd accepted the task and set to work did I find that an unlucky dip had led me to the only passage with which I *could* agree, and I didn't feel that having accepted I could back out. *Hinc illae lacrimae.*' ['Hence those tears', Terence, a Roman comic dramatist (c. 190–159 B.C), *Andria*, l. 126]. May Alfred and Fr Incledon both rest in peace.

APPENDIX III
The Marlborough Annulment

Thinking it best no longer to dissemble, I told her that I meant to marry X, adding that I considered I had a right to choose my own husband. These words, the bravest I had ever uttered, brought down a frightful storm of protest. I suffered every searing reproach, heard every possible invective, hurled at the man I loved. I was informed of his numerous flirtations, of his well-known love for a married woman, of his desire to marry an heiress. My mother even declared that he would have no children and that there was madness in the family. I had no answer to these accusations, but in my silence she must have read how obstinately I clung to my choice. In a final appeal to my feelings she argued that her decision to select a husband for me was founded on considerations I was too young and inexperienced to appreciate. Though rent by so emotional a plea, I still maintained my right to lead the life I wished. It was perhaps my unexpected resistance or the mere fact that no one had ever stood up to her that made her say she would not hesitate to shoot a man whom she considered would ruin my life.

We reached a stage where arguments were futile, and I left her then in the cold dawn of morning feeling as if all my life had been drained away. No one came near me and the morning dragged on its interminable course. I could not seek counsel with X, for there was no telephone. I could not write, for the servants had orders to bring my letters to my mother, neither could I get past the porter at the gate. The house was full of ominous rumours. I heard that my mother was ill and in her bed, that a doctor had been sent for; even my governess, usually so calm, was harassed. The suspense was becoming unbearable. There was no one I could consult; to appeal to my father, who was away at sea, and who knew nothing of my mother's schemes, would, I knew, only involve him in a hopeless struggle against impossible odds and further stimulate my mother's rancour.

> Later that day Mrs Jay, who was my mother's intimate friend and was staying with us at the time, came to talk to me. Condemning my behaviour, she told me that my mother had had a heart-attack brought about by my callous indifference to her feelings. She confirmed my mother's intentions of never consenting to my plans for marriage, and her resolve to shoot X should I decide to run away with him. I asked her whether I could see my mother and whether in her opinion she would ever relent. I still remember the terrible answer, 'Your mother will never relent, and I warn you there will be a catastrophe if you persist. The doctor has said that another scene may easily bring on a heart-attack and he will not be responsible for the result. You can ask the doctor yourself if you do not believe me!'
>
> Still under the strain of the painful scene with my mother, still seeing her frightening rage, it seemed to me that she might indeed easily suffer a stroke or a heart-attack if further provoked. In utter misery I asked Mrs Jay to let X know that I could not marry him.

[Shortly afterwards, she married the Duke, and writes of her wedding day]:

> Driving away from my home, I looked back. My mother was at the window. She was hiding behind a curtain, but I saw that she was in tears. 'And yet', I thought, 'she has attained the goal she set herself, she has experienced the satisfactions wealth can offer, she has ensconced me in the niche she early assigned me.' Consuelo Vanderbilt Balsan, *The Glitter and the Gold* (London: Heinemann, 1953), 42–43. Out of print, since reissued by St Martin's Press, 2012.

[Here follows her brief account of her second marriage and the annulment process of her first].

> Sanctified as our marriage had been in an Episcopal church, it was to me completely valid; and I would have been content to ignore the ultra-religious views that prevented the orthodox Catholics from recognising it. But in 1926, when Marlborough decided he wanted his first marriage annulled, the pressure brought by my French family and my desire to see Jacques at peace with them determined my decision to approach the Rota.

On consulting my English lawyer, Sir Charles Russell, a Catholic and a devoted friend, I found that my only valid claim to an annulment was the fact that I had been married against my will. It pained me to approach my mother for her consent, but on learning that the proceedings were entirely private, we agreed to take the necessary steps. The evidence once collected, I appeared before a tribunal of English priests versed in canonical law. My former governess, Miss Harper, gave valuable testimony, since she had personally witnessed the coercion to which I had been subjected. The application was then sent to the Rota, which granted the annulment.

All would have been well had not Marlborough gone to Rome to be received in audience by the Pope [Pius XI, reigned 6th February 1922–10th February 1939]. News of the annulment then got about and promptly unloosed a blast of Protestant wrath aimed at the Rota for annulling an Episcopal marriage. Alas, gone were our privacy and peace of mind as once again the Press exposed my story. My mother, with her usual courage, remained undaunted, but I suffered to see her in such an unfavourable light, knowing that she had hoped to ensure my happiness with the marriage she had forced upon me. Religious controversies are apt to be bitter; but there was no truth in the accusation that the Rota had been bribed. Counsels' fees and the cost of collecting evidence were the only disbursements and were much less than the charges of a legal divorce. It was, however, with some bitterness that I reflected that it had required three legal interventions to obtain my freedom, and then a fourth in the form of the Rota, each accompanied by an unpleasant and unnecessary publicity.

After the annulment was granted, I was married to Jacques in a Catholic ceremony and joined the family circle. The Balsans lived at Chateauroux in the centre of France. Their cloth factories had been founded by the Prince de Condé at the instigation of the minister, Colbert, who in the reign of Louis XIV reconstituted the commerce and industries of France. The family lived in the chateau and its dependencies, which were surrounded by park-like grounds; the factories were nearby.' Balsan, *The Glitter and the Gold*, 192–193.

APPENDIX IV
Humanae Vitae
POPE PAUL'S PROPHETIC WORDS

If there are reasonable grounds for spacing births, arising from the physical or psychological condition of husband or wife, or from external circumstances, the Church teaches that then married people may take advantage of the natural cycles immanent in the reproductive system and use their marriage at precisely those times that are infertile, and in this way control birth, a way which does not in the least offend the moral principles which we have just explained.

Neither the Church nor her doctrine is inconsistent when she considers it lawful for married people to take advantage of the infertile period but condemns as always unlawful the use of means which directly exclude conception, even when the reasons given for the latter practice are neither trivial nor immoral. In reality, these two cases are completely different. In the former married couples rightly use a facility provided them by nature. In the latter they obstruct the natural development of the generative process. It cannot be denied that in each case married couples, for acceptable reasons, are both perfectly clear in their intention to avoid children and mean to make sure that none will be born. But it is equally true that it is exclusively in the former case that husband and wife are ready to abstain from intercourse during the fertile period as often as for reasonable motives the birth of another child is not desirable. And when the infertile period recurs, they use their married intimacy to express their mutual love and safeguard their fidelity towards one another. In doing this they certainly give proof of a true and authentic love.

GRAVE CONSEQUENCES OF ARTIFICIAL BIRTH CONTROL

Responsible men can become more deeply convinced of the truth of the doctrine laid down by the Church on this issue if they reflect on the consequences of methods and plans for artificial restriction of increases in the birthrate. Let them first consider how easily this course of action can lead to the way being left wide open to marital infidelity and a general lowering of moral standards. Not much experience is needed to be fully aware of human weakness and to understand that men — and especially the young, who are so exposed to temptation — need incentives to keep the moral law, and it is an evil thing to make it easy for them to break that law. Another effect that gives cause for alarm is that a man who grows accustomed to the use of contraceptive methods may forget the reverence due to a woman, and, disregarding her physical and emotional equilibrium, reduce her to being a mere instrument for the satisfaction of his own desires, no longer considering her as his partner whom he should surround with care and affection.

Finally, grave consideration should be given to the danger of this power passing into the hands of those public authorities who care little for the precepts of the moral law. Who will blame a government which in its attempt to resolve the problems affecting an entire country resorts to the same measures as are regarded as lawful by married people in the solution of a particular family difficulty? Who will prevent public authorities from favouring those contraceptive methods which they consider more effective? Should they regard this as necessary, they may even impose their use on everyone. It could well happen, therefore, that when people, either individually or in family or social life, experience the inherent difficulties of the divine law and are determined to avoid them, they may be giving into the hands of public authorities the power to intervene in the most personal and intimate responsibility of husband and wife.

Consequently, unless we are willing that the responsibility of procreating life should be left to the arbitrary decision of men, we must accept that there are certain limits, beyond which it is wrong to go, to the power of man over his own body and its natural functions — limits, let it be said, which no one, whether as a private individual or as a public authority, can lawfully exceed. These limits are expressly imposed because of the reverence due to the whole human organism and its natural functions. Pope Saint Paul VI, *Humanae Vitae*, 'Lawfulness of recourse to infertile periods' (London: Incorporated Catholic Truth Society, 1968) par. 16–17.

Regarding UK government policy vis-a-vis contraception, child benefit has been limited by the Conservatives to a maximum of two children for those born after April 6, 2017. This policy was originally proposed by Catholic Conservative Iain Duncan Smith, as a way to help achieve the £12 billion in welfare cuts proposed by Conservative Chancellor of the Exchequer George Osborne. Duncan Smith's civil servants calculated it would save £1 billion a year. 'A source told *The Sunday Times:* "This will be about achieving behaviour change. With two children, you send a message where people have to think: 'Can I afford another child?'" Source: 'Downing Street rejects IDS plan for new limit on child benefit.' *The Guardian* (June 1, 2015).

Regarding 'behaviour change' since the contraceptive pill became commonplace in the early 1960s, with the 'sexual revolution' which it supercharged, infidelity increased as pregnancy was no longer the likely consequence of intercourse. Divorce rates consequently burgeoned, while newly legal abortions also multiplied, as unwanted pregnancies that had occurred in spite of contraceptive availability, were destroyed. Disrespect for women, one of the dangers predicted by Pope Paul, has certainly grown at the same time, both in terms of the loosening of censorship of pornography and its easy accessibility, with the consequent impact on male sexual behaviour and expectation of degrading or abuse-submissive conduct from their partners. Libby Purves summed it up in *The Times* when she said the Pill brought women more freedom but not more respect. Although touted as a liberator for women, it also freed men from responsibility, while coming with many side-effects.

Regarding those side-effects, a study in March 2023 found that the use of progesterone-only contraceptives was associated with a 20–30 percent higher risk of breast cancer. This was true for all forms of progesterone-containing contraceptives, whether patch, implant, coil or pill. An increased risk of blood-clots was also found, though this did not apply to progesterone-only products.[1] These physical dangers were not foreseen by Pope Paul. It is likely as a result of them that oral contraceptive use has more than halved, while Natural Family Planning (a method in tune with Catholic teaching) has nearly tripled in the last ten years.[2]

---

[1] Source: Laura Perrins, 'Pope Paul VI was right about The Pill—now everyone else is finally catching up.' *Catholic Herald*, April 20, 2023.

[2] Source: 'Davina McCall's Pill Revolution', Channel 4 programme, June 8, 2023.

APPENDIX V

Church Teaching & World Population
GOD'S TRUTH AND A PERSISTENT MYTH

HERE FOLLOWS A CATHOLIC DEFENCE OF Church teaching on contraception in the context of world population growth:

> ...CAFOD [The Catholic Fund for Overseas Development] acknowledges that the continuing rapid growth in the world's population has serious implications for Third World development. It poses a major challenge to the world community generally and to aid agencies in particular.
> ...Like most development NGOs (nongovernmental organisations), CAFOD believes that the principal cause of high birthrates is poverty. Reduced to a concise formula the solution is essentially: fewer people through less poverty, not less poverty through fewer people. The most important component of a population policy, therefore, is the sort of basic development programmes which enable people, and especially women, to see that they have some control over their lives, and which provide a level of security or safety-net which is otherwise provided at times of crisis and in old age by children. Wherever such sustained development has taken place, all the evidence suggests that people choose for themselves to have fewer children...
> CAFOD is committed to an integrated approach to development. It is opposed to strategies that concentrate on only one issue—such as population—giving credence to the widely held but mistaken belief that overpopulation is the single most important cause of poverty and environmental degradation. We believe that such strategies are not only misguided but harmful because they

divert people and resources from the structural changes needed to counter the growing impoverishment of much of the Third World and the ecological destruction that has come with it.

...CAFOD espouses the basic inalienable human right to marry, conceive and form a family where the decision as to the number of children should be a free, informed and responsible choice of both parents. CAFOD is utterly opposed to coercion from the state or any other body, and any measures which subvert the free choice of the couple. CAFOD warmly supports appropriate family planning education which enables properly informed decisions to be made — both about the spacing of children and about the number that can be economically supported.

...Family planning should take place within the cultural and religious context of people's understanding of sexuality and the family. CAFOD is opposed to anyone pursuing population programmes that do not respect the culture and beliefs of the people.

...In line with the norms of the Catholic Church, CAFOD does not finance programmes which promote the use of artificial contraceptives... (CAFOD Policy Statement: Population and Development)

The ICPD [UN International Conference on Population and Development] was organised to enable UN member states to consider population issues within the context of national goals for (i) sustained economic growth, (ii) sustainable human development, and (iii) improved education and economic status of women. They also discussed the proposal that the amount of aid allocated to population programmes and family planning should be tripled (from 1.4 to 4 percent of world aid). Many development agencies, including CAFOD, argue that, in the context of declining aid budgets, such an increase would inevitably be made at the expense of aid targeted at reducing poverty.

The ICPD was one of the most controversial and widely publicised UN conferences ever held and was the first time such issues were discussed at such a high-level global forum. The Conference ended with the adoption of a 113-page Programme of Action. Both the organisers

Appendix V

and governments congratulated themselves on its great success.

In contrast, many NGOs were disappointed that the Conference concentrated mainly on the issue of population and population control programmes rather than focusing on development. The media contributed to this by sensationalising controversies around family planning, diverting attention from the structural injustices behind poverty and the need for sustainable development.

... 'UN International Conference on Population and Development (ICPD), Cairo, September 1994', CAFOD Report with 'Policy Statement: Population and Development'.

World population is c. 8.2 billion at the time of writing (January 2025). Source: www.worldometers.info/world-population. It is currently expected to rise to 9.7 billion by 2050: source 'Coming of Age: Infographic on Global Population Trends', www.imf.org2020/03. Population growth is slowing from c. 1–2 percent to c. 0.5 percent annually, largely because of falling birth rates and an ageing population: source Pew Research Centre, analysis of U. N. World Population Prospects 2019 Report. This report finds that by 2050 global fertility is expected to be 2.2 births per woman, down from 2.5 today. This rate is 'inching closer to the replacement rate of 2.1 percent needed to maintain a population's size'.

CAFOD Report with 'Policy Statement: Population and Development', continues: The current [1994] debate about population growth is fuelled by concern for the environment. It tends, however, to overlook the fact that 20 percent of the world's population living in the industrialised North consume 80 percent of the world's resources.

South American rainforests are not being destroyed because Brazilians are having too many babies but because people in the North demand luxury furniture, fast food and cheap cars. UN conferences have consistently failed to address the issues of unsustainable consumerism and international economic policies (such as structural adjustment) which are widening the gap between rich and poor countries and rich and poor people within countries.

As Julian Filochowski, Director of CAFOD, says: 'It must be ironic to the people of the South that a group of Northern governments is scheming through the Cairo Conference to establish the right to abortion as a basic human right, and stands ready to provide the money to make it a reality when the most basic rights of all — to food, water, shelter, health care, education — enshrined by the UN half a century ago, are further away than ever from being fulfilled.'

... Over the past twenty years birth-rates have fallen from 2.6 to 1.8 births per woman in the North, and from between 5–7 children to 3–6 children in the South...

The World Bank has increased its spending on population programmes from $500 million in 1990 to $2.5 billion in 1995, whilst at the same time imposing structural adjustment programmes on countries, resulting in massive cuts in primary health care, education and other social services.

'UN International Conference on Population and Development (ICPD), Cairo, September 1994', CAFOD Report with 'Policy Statement: Population and Development'.

The above reports give the lie to screaming headlines like that in *The Daily Express* on September 3, 1998: 'TIMEBOMB — by 2000, there will be six billion people alive and the figure could double by 2050. How will we feed them all?' This was how the paper covered a UN report that 'the number of people in the world is rising at a rate of more than 220,000 a day... Earth's resources would be placed under tremendous strain.'

However, as a piece in *The Daily Telegraph* pointed out shortly afterwards:

As misleading reporting goes, this takes some beating. The UN report is optimistic in tone. It stresses that the rate of population growth is slowing; it has slowed so much and so unexpectedly that predictions made just a generation ago have proved badly wrong. The 6 billion mark has been much delayed. Ten years ago [i.e. 1988] we were told to expect 12 billion people by 2050; now 8 billion looks more likely [at time of writing actually 9.7 billion, based on most recent UN figures].

Appendix V

But the most misleading part is the implication that austerity and pain are the answers. The proven cure for population growth is prosperity and health, not coercion, starvation and self-denial.

There are three myths about population growth: first, that it is accelerating — the rate has been decelerating since 1960 (from 2 percent a year to 1.4 percent now) [more accurately, from 1964, when it was 2.25 percent; it is actually 0.85 percent per year at time of writing (January 2025, down from 0.97 percent in 2020, and 1.25 percent in 2015). Source: https://www.worldometers.info/world-population/]; second, that it is bad for the economy, when rising populations have usually meant growing prosperity both for particular countries and for the whole world; third, that it causes starvation and other forms of scarcity. Matt Ridley, 'Winning the Human Numbers Game', *Daily Telegraph* (September 1998).

It is ironic that *The Daily Express*'s entry in *The Writers' and Artists' Yearbook* (2015 edition) includes the statement: 'facts preferred to opinions.'

PRO-ABORTION MPS IGNORANT; UN ADMITS MISTAKE ON GROWTH RATE

For examples of the misleading presentation of the issue by pro-abortionists, one need look no further than a debate in the House of Commons on the topic shortly after the Earth Summit in New York, June 1997:

> 'Most of the claims in pro-abortion speeches throughout... showed an alarming ignorance of demographic and economic development' [stated Brendan Gerard, then SPUC Information Officer, who represented the International Right to Life Federation at the Earth Summit]. They also totally ignored the fact that the rate of world population growth was reported in May [1997] to be declining even more than the UN's lowest projection to date. Indeed, the head of the UN Population Fund was made to acknowledge this point when questioned by a journalist at the Earth Summit in New York.' *Human Concern* (SPUC Pro-life Newspaper), Autumn 1997.

This report, being contemporaneous with my interview with Alfred, refers to figures admittedly some 27 years old, but, as reported above, although world population continues to increase, the current, recent and overall trend in the growth rate is continually downwards, as it has been, with only slight occasional hiccups upwards, since 1964.

STATE COERCION: POPE PAUL PROVES PROPHETIC

Just six years after [Pope Paul VI warned in *Humanae Vitae* that one of the likely future consequences of the widespread acceptance of artificial contraception might be the enforcement of contraceptive methods upon people by their governments], in December 1974, the National Security Council of the United States completed a study entitled Implications of Worldwide Population Growth for U. S. Security and Overseas Interests — known in short as NSSM 200... NSSM 200 was a study promoted and endorsed by Henry Kissinger, President Nixon's National Security advisor, who pressed the need, in his own words, for 'U. S. leadership in world population matters' and urged for 'strong emphasis' on motivating leaders of 'key developing countries' to accept family planning activities. NSSM 200 expressed the gravest fears that the 'political consequences of current population factors in the less developed countries' might create 'political or even national security problems for the U. S.'

'The U. S. can help to minimise charges of an imperialist motivation behind its support of population activities by repeatedly asserting that such support derives from a concern with: (a) the right of the individual to determine freely and responsibly the number and spacing of children... and (b) the fundamental economic and social development of poor countries.'

In addition... NSSM 200 includes an 'alternative' viewpoint which holds that 'mandatory programmes may be needed and that we should be considering these possibilities now'. Questions included in such a viewpoint were: 'Would food be considered an instrument of national power? Will we be forced to make choices as to whom we can reasonably assist, and if so, should population effort be a criterion for such assistance?'

Appendix V

According to the 1984 World Bank Report Population Change and Economic Development... in Korea, free medical care and educational allowances were given to two-child families provided one of the parents had been sterilised; in Thailand technical assistance in farm production and marketing is made available to contraceptive users, and in India, women working on tea plantations received an extra day's pay for every month they were not pregnant... And in China current 'coercive' population control measures listed in a Shanghai social science journal in August 1989 included 'knocking down houses, felling trees, confiscating... cattle, tractors and other large equipment.'...

In 1983, as the one-child programme became increasingly coercive, the China Family Planning Association became a fully-fledged affiliate of the International Planned Parenthood Federation, which discussed in its magazine *People* (10:1 [1983]: 24) whether the Chinese programme might be a 'Third World Model.' The Chinese government in its turn has expressed profound gratitude to the International Planned Parenthood Federation for its help — in its national report for the Cairo Conference, 56–57. John Smeaton, 'Population and Development: Catholic Teaching', *Faith* magazine (September 1996). Smeaton was then CEO of SPUC (The Society for the Protection of Unborn Children).

BIBLIOGRAPHY

BOOKS BY ALFRED GILBEY, AND BOOKS IN WHICH HE IS FEATURED

Atallah, Naim. *Singular Encounters.* London: Quartet Books, 1990. Contains an interview, out of print, available online: https://quartetbooks.wordpress.com/2010/06/28/no-longer-with-us-monsignor-gilbey/.

Gilbey, Alfred. *We Believe.* Leominster: Gracewing, 2011.

——. *The Commonplace Book of Monsignor A. N. Gilbey.* London: Bellew Publishing, 1993.

Gregory-Jones, Peter. *A History of the Cambridge Catholic Chaplaincy 1895–1965.* Cagliari: Societa Poligrafica Sarda, 1986.

Watkin, David, ed. *Alfred Gilbey: A Memoir by Some Friends.* Norwich: Michael Russell Publishing Ltd, 2001.

PERIODICALS AND NEWSPAPERS CONTAINING INTERVIEWS WITH ALFRED GILBEY, REVIEWS OF HIS BOOKS, & OBITUARIES

Anonymous. 'Monsignor Alfred Gilbey 1901–1998'. Obituary, *The Catholic Herald.* April 3, 1998.

Anonymous, with addendum by David Watkin. 'Monsignor Alfred Gilbey'. Obituary. *The Daily Telegraph.* March 27, 1998.

Anonymous. 'Monsignor Alfred Gilbey'. Obituary. *The Times.* March 27, 1998.

Anonymous. 'Sad loss of a great priest'. Obituary. *Westminster Record.* April 1998.

Haydon, Alexander 'The old man of the century'. *The Catholic Herald.* April 12, 1996. Quoted by permission of *The Catholic Herald.*

Heim, Bruno B. Untitled review of *We Believe. Osservatore Romano.* March 26, 1984.

Incledon, Richard. 'Firm instructions'. Review of *We Believe. Times Literary Supplement.* September 21, 1984.

Mortimer, John. 'The Monsignor at Ninety', *Spectator.* July 6, 1991. http://archive.spectator.co.uk/article/6th-july-1991/19/the-monsignor-at-ninety.

Richard, Michael. 'Author in distress'. Review of *We Believe. The Tablet.* May 5, 1984.

BOOKS ON CATHOLICISM QUOTED OR CITED IN THE TEXT OR NOTES, IN ADDITION TO *WE BELIEVE* & *THE PENNY CATECHISM*

Compendium of the Catechism of the Catholic Church. London: Geoffrey Chapman, 2006.

John Paul II. *Crossing the Threshold of Hope.* London: Jonathan Cape, 1994.
Newman, John Henry. *Apologia Pro Vita Sua.* London: Sheed & Ward, 1976.
——. *The Idea of a University Defined and Illustrated.* Oxford, Oxford University Press, 1976.
Paul VI. *Humanae Vitae.* London: Catholic Truth Society, 1968.

BOOKS ON CHURCH AND SECULAR HISTORY FOR REFERENCE, AND THOSE QUOTED IN THE APPENDICES

Balsan, Consuelo Vanderbilt. *The Glitter and the Gold.* London: William Heinemann Ltd 1952. Out of print. Second edition: St Martin's Press, 2012.
Castleden, Rodney, *British History,* London: Parragon Book Service Ltd, 1994.
Farmer, David. *The Oxford Dictionary of Saints.* Oxford: Oxford University Press, 1992.
Holmes, Derek J. *The Papacy in the Modern World 1914–78.* London: Burns & Oates, 1981, out of print. This is an excellent one-volume summary that gives defenders of the Faith solid historical ammunition with which to defend Holy Mother Church against many of the usual slanders.
Hood, Harold, ed. *The Catholic Who's Who 1952.* London: Burns & Oates, 1952.
Hunt, Felicity and Carol Barker. *Women at Cambridge: A Brief History.* Cambridge: Cambridge University Press, 1998.
Kelly, J. N. D. *The Oxford Dictionary of Popes.* Oxford: Oxford University Press, 1986.
McWilliams-Tullberg, Rita, *Women at Cambridge: A Men's University — Though of a Mixed Type,* London: Victor Gollancz, 1975.
Preston, Paul. *Franco.* London: Fontana Press, 1993.

LITERARY WORKS & OTHER WORKS OF REFERENCE

Eliot, George, *The Mill on the Floss,* Oxford: Oxford University Press, 2015.
Hopkins, Gerard Manley, *Selected Poetry,* Oxford: Oxford University Press, 2008.
Knowles, Elizabeth, ed., *Oxford Dictionary of Quotations,* 6th Edition, Oxford: Oxford University Press, 2004.
Milton, John, *Paradise Lost,* Oxford: Oxford University Press, 2008.
Owen, Alysoun, ed., *The Writers' and Artists' Yearbook,* London: Bloomsbury, 2015.

Bibliography

OTHER ARTICLES QUOTED

Anonymous. 'Downing Street rejects IDS plan for new limit on child benefit', *The Guardian*, June 1, 2015.

Anonymous. 'Heirs and Disgraces', additional research by Sally Narraway, *The Guardian*, August 11, 1999.

Anonymous. https://www.sexeducationforum.org.uk/about/our-history-30-years-campaigning

Anonymous. 'Oxford & Cambridge Club Elects First Female Member', *The Chronicle of Higher Education*, April 12, 1996.

Anonymous. 'TIMEBOMB—by 2000, there will be six billion people alive and the figure could double by 2050.' *The Daily Express*, September 3, 1998.

Aston, Jennifer. 'EXPERT COMMENT: A Very British Scandal: divorce courts have been shaming women since the 1800s', https://newsroom.northumbria.ac.uk/pressreleases/expert-comment-a-very-british-scandal-divorce-courts-have-been-shaming-women-since-the-1800s-3156137, Press Release of January 19, 2022.

Atallah, Naim. 'Frances Partridge', Naim Atallah Online, an interview, https://quartetbooks.wordpress.com/2014/08/15/frances-partridge/, posted August 15, 2014.

Author and title not recorded. [Report on 1920 vote to admit women as equal members of Cambridge University], *CAM* (Cambridge Alumni Magazine), Easter Term 1998.

Author not recorded. 'UN International Conference on Population and Development (ICPD), Cairo, September 1994', CAFOD Report, September 1994.

Author not recorded. CAFOD Policy Statement: 'Population and Development'. Year of publication unknown; probably 1990s.

Bencharif, Sara-Taissir, https://www.politico.eu/article/meps-vote-for-abortion-rights-to-be-in-eu-charter-of-fundamental-rights/, *Politico*, July 7, 2022.

Caron, Paul L, https://taxprof.typepad.com/taxprof_blog/2017/09/bainbridge-is-tax-avoidance-immoral-a-catholic-perspective.html, Tax Prof Blog, Caruso School of Law, September 10, 2017.

Cilluffo, Anthony & Ruiz, Neil G, 'World's population is projected to nearly stop growing by the end of the century', Pew Research Centre, June 17, 2019.

David-Barrett, T., *Women Favour Dyadic Relationships, but Men Prefer Clubs: Cross-Cultural Evidence from Social Networking*, National Library of Medicine, March 16, 2015.

Gerard, Brendan. Report on House of Commons Debate After 1997 Earth Summit, *Human Concern*, Autumn 1997.

Lucie-Smith, Alexander, 'Fr Charles-Roux: He loved the Mass, he loved

God. May he now enjoy the vision of God forever', *Catholic Herald* August 11, 2014, by permission of the *Catholic Herald*.

Massingberd, Hugh. 'The eccentricities of Monsignor Gilbey', review of *Alfred Gilbey: A Memoir by Some Friends*, David Watkin, ed., *Spectator*, March 16, 2002.

Perrins, Laura, 'Pope Paul VI was right about the Pill—now everyone else is finally catching up', *The Catholic Herald*, April 20, 2023. By permission of *The Catholic Herald*.

Ridley, Matt. 'Winning the Human Numbers Game', *The Daily Telegraph* September 1998.

Smeaton, John. 'Population and Development: Catholic Teaching', *Faith* magazine, September 1996.

Thompson, Damian, 'Jean-Marie Charles-Roux, a good and holy priest,' *The Spectator*, August 8, 2014.

www.ingramcontent.com/pod-product-compliance
Ingram Content Group UK Ltd.
Pitfield, Milton Keynes, MK11 3LW, UK
UKHW022112200725
461008UK00008B/126